ADULT READING SERIES

Challenger

Teacher's Manual

FOR BOOK 5

COREA MURPHY

About the Author

Corea Murphy has worked in the field of education since the early 1960s. In addition to classroom and tutorial teaching, Ms. Murphy has developed language arts curriculum guides for public high schools, conducted curriculum and effectiveness workshops, and established an educational program for residents in a drug rehabilitation facility.

Ms. Murphy became interested in creating a reading series for older students when she began working with illiterate adults and adolescents in the early 1970s. The **Challenger Adult Reading Series** is the result of her work with these students.

In a very real sense, these students contributed greatly to the development of this reading series. Their enthusiasm for learning to read and their willingness to work hard provided inspiration, and their many helpful suggestions influenced the content of both the student books and the teacher's manuals.

It is to these students that the **Challenger Adult Reading Series** is dedicated with the hope that others who wish to become good readers will find this reading program both helpful and stimulating.

A special note of gratitude is also extended to Kay Koschnick, Christina Jagger, and Mary Hutchison of New Readers Press for their work and support in guiding this series to completion.

ISBN 0-88336-875-7

EACH ONE TEACH ONE

© 1991
New Readers Press
Publishing Division of Laubach Literacy International
Box 131, Syracuse, New York 13210

Printed in the United States of America

Cover design by Chris Steenwerth

9 8 7 6 5 4 3 2

Table of Contents

Introduction to the *Challenger* Series

Challenger Adult Reading Series is an eight-book program of reading, writing, and reasoning skills designed to meet the needs of adult and adolescent students. It takes students from the beginning stages of reading to the critical reading, writing, and reasoning skills associated with the latter ninth grade level. The first four books in this series emphasize "learning to read." Beginning with the fifth book, the emphasis shifts to "reading to learn."

Each book in this controlled vocabulary series contains twenty lessons, plus reviews. Each lesson includes a reading selection and a variety of exercises and activities.

The reading selections in the odd-numbered books are generally fiction pieces. Books 1 and 3 contain light-hearted stories about adult characters who get caught up in a variety of situations. Most reading selections in Books 5 and 7 are minimally adapted well-known works of fiction.

The reading selections in the even-numbered books are engaging nonfiction pieces. The selections in Books 2 and 4 are generally similar to topics found in encyclopedias. Most selections in Books 6 and 8 are adaptations from highly-respected works of nonfiction. These selections enable students to broaden the scope of their knowledge.

Preceding each reading selection in the odd-numbered books is a word chart that introduces new words according to a specific phonics principle. In Books 1 and 3, these words appear frequently in both the reading selections and the exercises. In Books 5 and 7, the words from these charts are the basis for dictionary work and other word study exercises.

The wide variety of exercises and activities helps students develop their reading, writing, and reasoning skills and increase their basic knowledge. Comprehension exercises based on the reading selections focus on the development of literal, inferential, and critical reading skills. Also, the comprehension exercises in Books 5 through 8 introduce or reinforce various concepts associated with literary understanding.

Word study exercises are designed to increase the students' vocabulary and further develop their reading and reasoning skills. These exercises vary from simple word associations to classifying, sequencing, and categorizing exercises, analogies, vocabulary reviews, activities which emphasize using context clues, those which require using dictionaries and other reference materials, and several types of puzzles.

Students are eased into writing. Early in the series, exercises focus on writing at the sentence level and are designed to simultaneously improve spelling, sentence structure, and students' skill in expressing themselves clearly. Most lessons in Books 5 through 8 include at least one exercise in which the student must write responses in complete sentences or brief paragraphs. The individual lesson notes in this manual offer suggestions of topics to be considered for additional writing assignments. Although *Challenger* is primarily a reading series, teachers should encourage their students to understand that writing is an essential aspect of literacy.

The review lessons of Books 1 through 5 contain indexes of the words introduced in the preceding lessons. Word indexes are included in the Teacher's Manuals for Books 6 through 8. These indexes can be used in developing various reinforcement activities and vocabulary reviews.

The books also include periodic reviews. The last review in each book can be used as a diagnostic tool to determine the appropriate placement for students using this program. An accuracy rate of 85% or better on the final reviews indicates that a student is ready for the next book.

Significant Educational Features

Wide Learning Suitability/ Minimal Instructional Needs

This series has been tested successfully with students in many different types of instructional settings:

- Secondary remedial reading programs
- Secondary special education programs
- Adult volunteer literacy programs
- ABE, pre-GED, and GED programs
- Community college reading programs
- Educational programs in correctional institutions
- Tutorial programs for employees who wish to develop literacy skills in order to advance in their chosen occupations

Because both adults and older teens develop their skills more effectively when they assume a high degree of responsibility for their learning development, the lessons in the *Challenger* series have been designed so that they can be completed by students with only minimal instruction from the teacher.

An Integrated Approach

These books integrate reading, writing, and reasoning activities. The words introduced in each lesson provide the organizing principle for this integration. Through frequently seeing and using these words in reading, writing, and reasoning activities which are repeated in design but varied in content, students are better able to understand and apply what they have learned to a variety of situations. The thoroughness of this integrated approach enables students to begin each new lesson with greater mastery and confidence.

Sequenced Skill Building

Each lesson builds upon skills and content which students have worked with in previous lessons. Students experience a sense of progress because they quickly learn to apply their skills to new situations.

Students are continually challenged by the increased breadth and difficulty of each lesson, through which their reading progress is reflected. Generally, each reading selection is slightly longer than the previous one. In addition, the content, vocabulary, and sentence structure in the reading selections gradually become more sophisticated and demanding. The exercises, too, capitalize on students' increasing proficiency. Building on students' current skill level, the exercises gradually expand the students' knowledge in a spiral-like fashion—both broadening and deepening their abilities in the various skill areas.

Highly Motivating Material

For the past ten years, this series has been used with adult and adolescent populations for which it is designed. Students comment that many characteristics of this reading program help to hold their interest in their efforts to become more proficient readers. The characteristics they most frequently cite include:

- the exceptionally motivating reading selections
- the mature presentation and diversity of material
- the information presented in each lesson
- the emphasis on using reasoning powers
- the challenge of increasingly difficult materials
- the success and confidence the *Challenger* books generate

Comprehensive Teacher's Manuals

The comprehensive teacher's manuals offer practical suggestions about procedures and techniques for working with students. Individual lesson notes in the manuals present objectives, guidelines, and suggestions for specific activities in each lesson.

Answer Keys

Complete answer keys for each lesson in the first four books are found in both the *Teacher's Manual for Books 1-4* and in the *Answer Key for Books 1-4*. The *Answer Key for Books 5-8* contains the answers for those books. In addition, the individual teacher's manuals for *Challenger* 5, 6, 7, and 8 contain answer keys for each of those books.

> Although it is recognized that there are students of both sexes, for the sake of clarity and simplicity, we chose to use the pronouns *he, him,* and *his* throughout this book.

SCOPE AND SEQUENCE: BOOK 5

Phonics

Lesson	1	2	3	4	R	5	6	7	8	R	9	10	11	12	R	13	14	15	16	R	17	18	19	20	R
1. Use phonics skills to decode unknown words	★	★	★	★	★	★	★	★	★	★	★	★	★	★	★	★	★	★	★	★	★	★	★	★	★
2. Recognize long and short vowel sounds	☆	★	☆	★	★	★	★	★	★	★	★	★	★	★	★	★	★	★	★	★	★	★	★	★	☆
3. Recognize sounds for consonant blends	☆	★	☆	★	☆	★	★	★	☆	☆	☆	☆	☆	☆	☆	☆	☆	☆	☆	☆	☆	☆	☆	☆	☆
4. Recognize sounds for digraphs	☆	☆	☆	☆	☆	☆	☆	☆	☆	☆	☆	☆	☆	☆	☆	☆	☆	☆	☆	☆	☆	☆	☆	☆	☆
5. Recognize sounds for vowel combinations	☆	☆	☆	☆	☆	☆	☆	☆	☆	☆	★	☆	☆	☆	☆	☆	☆	☆	☆	☆	☆	☆	☆	☆	☆
6. Recognize sounds for r-controlled vowels	☆	☆	☆	☆	☆	☆	☆	☆	☆	☆	☆	☆	★	☆	☆	☆	☆	☆	☆	☆	☆	☆	☆	☆	☆
7. Recognize sounds for c	☆	☆	☆	☆	☆	☆	☆	☆	☆	☆	☆	☆	☆	☆	☆	☆	☆	☆	☆	☆	☆	☆	☆	☆	☆
8. Identify sounds for c													☆												
9. Recognize sounds for g	☆	☆	☆	☆	☆	☆	☆	☆	☆	☆	☆	☆	☆	☆	☆	☆	☆	☆	☆	☆	☆	☆	☆	☆	☆
10. Identify sounds for g												☆		☆											
11. Recognize sounds for y	☆	☆	☆	☆	☆	☆	☆	☆	☆	☆	☆	☆	☆	☆	☆	☆	☆	☆	☆	☆	☆	☆	☆	☆	☆
12. Recognize the sound for ph																							★		
13. Contrast sounds								☆	☆	☆					☆					☆	☆			☆	☆

Word Analysis

Lesson	1	2	3	4	R	5	6	7	8	R	9	10	11	12	R	13	14	15	16	R	17	18	19	20	R
1. Use syllabication to decode words	★	★	★	★	★	★	★	★	★	★	★	★	★	★	★	★	★	★	★	★	★	★	★	★	★
2. Divide words into syllables	☆		☆	☆	☆	☆					☆	☆				☆	☆	☆	☆		☆	☆	☆		☆
3. Form compound words							☆	☆	☆		☆								☆						
4. Recognize common word beginnings: re-																									
pre-, per-								☆						☆											
dis-											☆		☆												
5. Recognize common word endings: -er																									
-y									☆	☆						☆									
-ment																			☆						
-ness																		☆							
-ful, -less														☆							★				
el, ture, ale																						☆	☆		
le, al, et, tion, sion, ish															☆				☆	☆	★				
et, age, ice, ive																				☆	☆				

Vocabulary

Lesson	1	2	3	4	R	5	6	7	8	R	9	10	11	12	R	13	14	15	16	R	17	18	19	20	R
1. Learn unfamiliar vocabulary	★	★	★	★	★	★	★	★	★	★	★	★	★	★	★	★	★	★	★	★	★	★	★	★	★
2. Infer word meanings from context clues	★	★	★	★	★	★	★	★	★	★	★	★	★	★	★	★	★	★	★	★	★	★	★	★	★
3. Identify definitions/descriptions of terms	★	★	★	★	★	★	★	★	★	★	★	★	★	★	★	★	★	★	★	★	★	★	★	★	★
4. Complete word associations	☆					☆								☆											
5. Identify synonyms		☆	☆	☆	☆				☆	☆					☆		☆	☆	☆			☆		☆	☆
6. Identify antonyms			☆	☆	☆		☆			☆					☆	☆	☆	☆			☆			★	★
7. Identify multiple meanings of words			☆										☆		☆								☆		
8. Complete analogies					☆			☆								★				☆					
9. Learn/review idiomatic expressions/common sayings					☆						☆			☆	★	☆							☆		
10. Complete puzzles (double crostics and cryptograms)															☆										

KEY: ★ = Primary emphasis   ★ = Secondary emphasis   ☆ = Integrated with other skills

Comprehension

Lesson	1	2	3	4	R	5	6	7	8	R	9	10	11	12	R	13	14	15	16	R	17	18	19	20	R
1. Identify words using context clues	★	★	★	★		★	★	★	★	★	★	★	★	★		★	★	★	★		★	★	★	★	★
2. Read stories independently		★	★	★		★	★	★	★		★	★	★	★		★	★	★	★		★	★	★	★	★
3. Complete exercises independently	★	★	★	★	★	★	★	★	★	★	★	★	★	★	★	★	★	★	★	★	★	★	★	★	★
4. Improve listening comprehension	☆	☆	☆	☆	☆	☆	☆	☆	☆	☆	☆	☆	☆	☆	☆	☆	☆	☆	☆	☆	☆	☆	☆	☆	☆
5. Group words appropriately when reading orally	☆	☆	☆	☆	☆	☆	☆	☆	☆	☆	☆	☆	☆	☆	☆	☆	☆	☆	☆	☆	☆	☆	☆	☆	☆
6. Interpret punctuation correctly when reading orally	☆	☆	☆	☆	☆	☆	☆	☆	☆	☆	☆	☆	☆	☆	☆	☆	☆	☆	☆	☆	☆	☆	☆	☆	☆
7. Develop literal comprehension skills:																									
– Recall details	★	★	★	★	★	★	★	★	★	★	★	★	★	★	★	★	★	★	★	★	★	★	★	★	★
– Locate specific information	★	★	★	★	★	★	★	★	★	★	★	★	★	★	★	★	★	★	★	★	★	★	★	★	★
– Identify cause and effect relationships	★	★								★			★	★					★						
– Recall sequence of events																		★	★			★			
8. Develop inferential comprehension skills:																									
– Infer word meanings from context clues	★	★	★	★		★	★	★	★	★	★	★	★	★		★	★	★	★		★	★	★	★	
– Infer information from the story	★	★	★	★		★	★	★	★		★	★	★	★		★	★	★	★		★	★	★	★	★
– Use context clues to predict correct responses	★	★	★	★	★	★	★	★	★		★	★	★	★	★	★	★	★	★	★	★	★	★	★	★
– Draw conclusions based on story	★		☆						☆					★		★	★		★		★	★			
– Infer cause and effect relationships		★					★			★							★				★	★			
– Classify words under topic headings													☆			☆			☆						
9. Develop applied comprehension skills:																									
– Relate reading to personal experience		★	★	★			★						★				★	★					★		
– Draw conclusions based on personal experience					★	★			★	★	★														
10. Learn/review basic factual information									★								★					★	★	★	
11. Locate/infer information from a circle graph									☆														☆		

Literary understanding

Lesson	1	2	3	4	R	5	6	7	8	R	9	10	11	12	R	13	14	15	16	R	17	18	19	20	R
1. Identify/interpret characters' actions, motivations, feelings, and qualities	★	★	★	★		★	★	★	★		★	★	★	★		★	★	★	★		★	★	★	★	★
2. Identify/interpret plot	★	★	★	★	★	★	★	★	★	★	★	★	★	★	★	★	★	★	★	★	★	★	★	★	★
3. Identify/interpret setting (time and/or place)	★	★	★	★		★					★	★				★	★		★			★	★		
4. Identify/infer narrator	★																								
5. Relate characters' names to qualities			★									★													
6. Create ending for story					★																				
7. Relate to characters' motivations and feelings							★		★		★		★							★				★	
8. Identify theme														★		★		★			★				
9. Predict outcome of story								★	★			★						★					★	★	
10. Recognize personification								★	★										★						
11. Identify surprise ending											★														
12. Recognize biography												★													
13. Recognize fables																★									
14. Infer moral or fable																★									
15. Contrast stories																		★							
16. Recognize autobiography																		★							
17. Infer narrator's attitude toward character																					★				
18. Identify tone																							★		

KEY: ★ = Primary emphasis   ☆ = Secondary emphasis   ☆ = Integrated with other skills

Writing

Lesson	1	2	3	4	R	5	6	7	8	R	9	10	11	12	R	13	14	15	16	R	17	18	19	20	R
1. Copy words accurately	★	★	★	★	★	★	★	★	★	★	★	★	★	★	★	★	★	★	★	★	★	★	★	★	★
2. Capitalize words appropriately	★	★	★	★	★	★	★	★	★	★	★	★	★	★	★	★	★	★	★	★	★	★	★	★	★
3. Spell words with greater accuracy	★	★	★	★	★	★	★	★	★	★	★	★	★	★	★	★	★	★	★	★	★	★	★	★	★
4. Form new words by adding the ending -*y*																☆									
5. Change the *y* to *i* before adding -*ness*																		☆							
6. Change dialect to standard English																			☆						
7. Use homonyms correctly																			☆						☆
8. Write sentence or paragraph answers to questions		★	★	★		★	★	★	★		★		★			★	★	★	★	★	★		★	★	★

Note: Specific suggestions for additional writing assignments appear in the individual lesson notes for Book 5 and in Chapter 7 of this manual.

Study Skills

Lesson	1	2	3	4	R	5	6	7	8	R	9	10	11	12	R	13	14	15	16	R	17	18	19	20	R
1. Increase concentration	★	★	★	★	★	★	★	★	★	★	★	★	★	★	★	★	★	★	★	★	★	★	★	★	★
2. Skim story to locate information	★	★	★	★	★	★	★	★	★		★	★	★	★	★	★	★	★	★	★	★	★	★	★	★
3. Use a dictionary to look up word meanings	★	★	★	★	★	★	★	★	★	★	★	★	★	★	★	★	★	★	★	★	★	★	★	★	★
4. Apply reasoning skills to exercises: context clues	★	★	★	★	★	★	★	★	★	★	★	★	★	★	★	★	★	★	★	★	★	★	★	★	★
process of elimination	★	★	★	★	★	★	★	★	★	★	★	★	★	★	★	★	★	★	★	★	★	★	★		★
"intelligent guessing"	★	★	★	★		★								★											

KEY: ★ = Primary emphasis   ☆ = Secondary emphasis   ☆ = Integrated with other skills

1. Introduction to Book 5

The format of Book 5 corresponds to the one used in earlier odd-numbered books in the *Challenger* series. Each lesson begins with a word chart that introduces words into this controlled-vocabulary series according to specific phonics principles. The sound for *ph*, introduced in Lesson 19, is the only phonics principle that students are studying for the first time in this series.

Definitions of difficult words from the word chart appear in a matching exercise that immediately follows each word chart. All students should own or have access to a dictionary in order to complete these exercises. Dictionary work is more heavily emphasized in Book 5 than in earlier books in this series.

The reading selections in Book 5 are adaptations of well-known and well-written literary pieces. With five exceptions, all the adaptations are from short stories. You should point out to students that they are reading quality literature. Experience indicates that students' self-esteem and motivation are bolstered when they realize that they are studying widely-acclaimed authors.

The exercises and reviews in Book 5 help the students to develop further their comprehension skills, recall, and reasoning abilities. Literary understanding is emphasized in the reading comprehension exercises. In addition, the concepts *synonym, antonym,* and *homonym* are introduced in Book 5.

A review appears after every four lessons. These reviews provide students with additional opportunities to review words and concepts. They also help students to develop the habit of referring to previous lessons for the correct answers to some of the questions. At the end of the reviews are word indexes containing the words introduced so far in Book 5. These indexes can be used when developing reinforcement activities such as spelling and vocabulary reviews.

Book 5 is the appropriate starting point for students who score in the 5.0-6.5 range on standardized reading achievement tests. The final review in Book 4 can also be used as a placement tool. An accuracy rate of 85% or better for this review indicates that students are ready for Book 5.

Students who start this series in Book 5 may need extensive oral reading practice because many students who begin work at this level are careless decoders. Their homework often reflects carelessness also. By calling students' attention to oral reading errors and conducting homework cri-

tiques, you can correct this pattern. All students who use this book should be given as many opportunities for oral reading practice as time permits. This practice helps to develop confidence, enjoyment, and interest in reading.

Book 5 builds upon procedures and practices emphasized in the earlier books in this series. Thus, you may find it worthwhile to look through the manual notes for some of these books.

Scheduling Considerations

Book 5 works well in a classroom setting. The most progress is achieved when students work with *Challenger* a minimum of 45 minutes two or three times a week. Students can work independently, in a group, or with a partner. When working with other students, they receive the support and stimulation from one another that makes learning more enjoyable. Also, the more advanced students can assume much of the responsibility for giving explanations and leading reinforcement activities, which in turn reinforces their own reading skills. Experience indicates that less advanced students usually benefit from peer instruction provided that you are available to supply any necessary clarifications.

The Lesson Components

Later chapters of this manual outline the principles and procedures that form the foundation of this reading series. The major components of the lessons in Book 5 are briefly described below.

Word Chart

Like the earlier odd-numbered books in this series, Book 5 uses common phonics principles to organize the introduction of new words. Words presented in this manner help students to understand better the many patterns that exist in the English language. This awareness, in turn, contributes to students' reading development. How much emphasis you place on the phonics principles reviewed in these word charts depends upon the pronunciation and spelling needs of your students.

Word Meanings

A matching exercise directly follows each word chart. Words in this exercise are taken from the word chart. Students are encouraged to use a dictionary for unfamiliar words. For this exercise, 100% accuracy is desired.

Words for Study

This section, which precedes the reading selection in each lesson, lists words in the lesson that appear for the first time in this series. As was the case in the earlier books, these words appear in the same order and form in which they initially appear in the lesson. This gives students additional practice in pronouncing word endings accurately.

Story

Most of the reading selections in Book 5 are short story adaptations. It is important for students to understand the differences between fiction and nonfiction. These terms should be introduced or reviewed. Familiarize students with the main elements in short fiction: character, setting, plot, and theme.

In addition to the adaptations of short stories, four other types of literature are presented: myth (Lesson 2), biography (Lesson 10), fables (Lesson 13), and autobiography (Lessons 15 and 16).

Introduce the reading selections with appropriate pre-reading activities, and try to link the readings with your students' prior knowledge and experiences whenever possible. It is also a good idea to give students a purpose for reading by setting a specific task for them to keep in mind as they are reading. The individual lesson notes contain some suggestions for pre-reading activities.

With the exception of the first lesson, students should read the selections as homework. Read the first few paragraphs of each selection aloud in class to acquaint students with the author's style and the tone of the selection. Follow this by asking one or two questions about what you read to be sure students understood it.

Have a brief general discussion of each reading selection after students have read it to give them a chance to react to it before discussing their responses to the comprehension questions.

About the Story

The comprehension questions in Book 5 are designed to move students beyond the level of literal comprehension and to help them develop inferential and critical comprehension skills. Most of the lessons contain questions on all three of these levels.

The comprehension exercises call for a variety of different responses: multiple choice, fill in the blank, and complete sentence responses. This variety gives students practice with formats that appear on both job-placement tests and the GED Test—tests that many students using this book may well encounter.

Other Exercises

A wide variety of exercises has been included to help students improve their recall, increase their vocabulary, and develop their reasoning abilities. As often as seems appropriate, draw students' attention to the fact that reasoning is an essential part of reading. Help them develop such strategies as using the process of elimination, making intelligent guesses, using the dictionary, and referring to previous lessons when completing these exercises.

A score of 80% or higher should be considered satisfactory on these exercises. If students consistently score below this figure, take some time to help them pinpoint the problem. Often they are trying to complete the exercises too rapidly.

Because students are encouraged to learn from their mistakes, they should not be penalized for making them. If you work in a school that gives report cards, it is strongly recommended that evaluations be based on corrected work and overall progress rather than on students' initial efforts. In no way does this practice encourage typical reading students to be careless in completing their homework. Rather, they usually become more interested in reading than in report cards, they are more relaxed and patient with themselves in completing assignments, and they develop a more realistic definition of academic progress.

Reinforcement Activities

Suggestions and procedures for reinforcement activities for those words and concepts that give students difficulty are discussed in Chapter 4.

Writing Assignments

Student writing is discussed in Chapter 5. It is recommended that students working in Book 5 complete weekly writing assignments of 100-125 words in addition to the writing that is required to complete the exercises in the individual lessons. Paragraphs or brief essays about discussion topics that interest students and personal and/or business letters are also appropriate writing assignments. Suggestions for writing assignments are also given in the individual lesson notes.

The Lesson Format

The procedure for each lesson should be as consistent as possible.

1. Students go over the writing assignment if one was given and review the work in the previous lesson first. This includes discussing the reading selection and correcting the exercises.

2. If time permits, students complete relevant reinforcement activities. The nature and scope of these activities are determined by the needs of your students and how often you meet with them.

3. Students preview the next lesson, which is usually assigned for homework.

Individual Lesson Notes

Lesson notes for each individual lesson appear in Chapter 7 of this manual. These notes contain suggestions and procedures for specific items in each lesson.

Answer Key

An answer key for the exercises in each lesson of Book 5 follows the individual lesson notes. However, interpretive questions often have more than one acceptable response. As a general rule, accept all answers that students can justify, even when they don't match the answers given in the answer key.

Word Indexes

The word indexes at the back of this manual contain lists of words that are introduced to this series in each unit of Book 5. There is also a master list of all the words introduced in this book. These lists are helpful when developing reinforcement activities.

The next three chapters give suggestions for preparing and teaching the lessons and selecting reinforcement activities.

2. Preparing to Teach

The following suggestions are based on the author's experiences and those of other teachers who have used these books. You may find that your own situation renders some of these suggestions either impractical or impossible to implement in your classroom. It is hoped, however, that most of these suggestions can be modified to meet your particular needs.

How Often to Use *Challenger*

In general, it is recommended that teachers use *Challenger* with students two or three times a week for at least 45 minutes per session. If you meet five times a week with pre-GED students who are eager to pass the tests and have time outside the classroom to complete homework assignments, you may want to use *Challenger* every day.

If you meet five times a week with an adult or adolescent reading class that does not have a specific task such as GED preparation to motivate them, the recommended schedule is to focus on the lessons three times a week and devote the other two class sessions to activities which reinforce or enrich material presented in the lessons. Suggestions about these reinforcement activities appear in Chapter 4.

It is important that students recognize the need to work with *Challenger* regularly. This is often an issue for students in volunteer programs or institutions in which class attendance is not mandatory. Whatever the situation, if a student chooses to attend class on a highly infrequent basis, tell him politely but frankly that there is little point in his attending at all because he's not giving himself a chance to make any significant progress.

If only one class meeting a week is possible, try to schedule this class for 90 minutes to two hours. Also, have the students complete two lessons and, if appropriate, a writing activity for homework. When the students look at you as if you were crazy, show them that by completing a few components of the lessons each day, they will not only be able to do the work, but also reinforce what they are learning. Sports and music are helpful analogies because most students know that both require daily practice.

The Lesson Format

After the first class, which of course involves no homework review, the procedure for each lesson is basically the same. The overview below gives you an idea of what happens during each class. More detailed procedures for this work appear in later chapters of this manual.

1. **Writing assignment.** If students have been given a writing assignment, begin the class by letting them share their work in pairs or small groups. Chapter 5 gives details on writing assignments.

2. **Homework review.** Discuss the reading selection to make sure students have understood it and to give them a chance to react to the reading. Then go over the comprehension questions and the other exercises and have students make any necessary corrections.

3. **Reinforcement activity.** If no writing assignment was given and if time permits, have the students do one or more reinforcement activities. See Chapter 4 for suggestions about reinforcement activities.

4. **Homework preview.** Go over the Words for Study listed at the beginning of the lesson. Introduce the reading selection and call attention to any special features that may be new or confusing. Have students quickly preview the individual exercises for anything they don't understand.

Following this general procedure on a fairly consistent basis helps students because they tend to feel more relaxed and work better when they have a sense of routine. Modifications in the procedure should be made only when they will enhance students' reading development.

Just as you encourage students to see homework assignments as daily workouts, encourage them to see class time as a daily workout, also. These lessons should not be seen as achievement tests but rather as opportunities to move students smoothly toward their reading goals. Students do not have to demonstrate mastery of the material in one lesson in order to go on to the next lesson. Mastery will come with consistent practice.

It is crucial for teachers to think in terms of improvement rather than mastery because students using these books often want to add a fourth component to the lesson format—rationalizing and/or lamenting their mistakes. This uses up valuable classroom time and, if allowed a foothold, will result in students' giving up and dropping out. Students must learn to perceive their mistakes as a natural and helpful part of the learning process. They can learn this only by your gentle but firm reminder that consistent practice is the key to mastery.

Remember that both adult and adolescent reading students tend to be overly sensitive to mistakes in their work. In most cases, they firmly believe that if they hadn't made so many mistakes in the first place, they wouldn't have to be working in these books. For example, a woman in her mid-twenties who decided to quit class explained her reason this way: "My teacher told me that it was all right to make mistakes, but every time I had one in my work she would kind of close her eyes and shake her head like I should have learned all this in the fourth grade." Teachers must think and act in terms of improvement rather than mastery and regard mistakes as natural and helpful.

Do not expect to know at the outset how much time to allot to each segment of the lesson. Understanding exactly how to pace the lessons takes time. By paying attention to students' responses and rate of accuracy, you will gradually learn how to schedule the lessons so that students improve their reading and writing skills in a relaxed but efficient manner.

Preparing the Lessons

In preparing the lessons, develop the habit of following this procedure:

1. Familiarize yourself with the lesson students are to work on that day.
2. Review the appropriate lesson notes in Chapter 7 of this manual for suggestions to help you teach the lesson. Go over the appropriate answers in the Answer Key as well.
3. Review any notes you took after the preceding class in which you jotted down vocabulary words or writing difficulties that students need to review. Teacher note-taking is discussed in Chapter 6 of this manual.
4. Decide upon any reinforcement activities you may want to use and complete any preparation needed. Suggestions for reinforcement activities are given in Chapter 4.
5. Skim the lesson to be assigned for homework and the appropriate lesson notes so you can introduce the reading selection and answer any questions students may have about the exercises.

Last and most important, you need to prepare yourself mentally and emotionally for the class. If possible, take several minutes before the students' arrival to unwind from the previous activities of the day. As a general rule, how well the lesson goes is determined by how relaxed and focused you are on the work. As the teacher, your main function is to serve as a smooth bridge between the student and the lesson material. Your own patience and concentration will determine how helpful this "bridge" is.

The Teacher-Student Relationship

Making sure that you are relaxed for the lesson also contributes to the development of a good working relationship with your students. Adolescent or adult reading students rely heavily on your support and encouragement.

It is helpful to remember that most of us, as we grow older, learn to fake or avoid situations in which we feel inadequate. We prefer habits and routines that are familiar and give us some sense of security. Adolescent or adult reading students have entered into a situation in which they can neither avoid (unless they give up) or fake their way through the material. They are to be admired for having put themselves in this situation. Unless they are extremely motivated or thick-skinned, they must feel a sense of support from you or they will eventually drop out, because exposing their lack of knowledge just gets too painful after a while.

In addition, completing the lessons in these books *is* hard work. No matter how much progress is being made, virtually all students experience a sense of frustration at one time or another. Your encouragement will help them to get through these gloomy periods when they are ready to throw in the towel.

Suggestions for a Good Working Rapport

The following are suggestions to help you consider how best to develop a good working relationship with your students.

- Strive for naturalness in your voice and mannerisms. Some teachers unconsciously treat reading students as if they were mental invalids or victims of a ruthless society. A condescending or pitying approach does not help students become better readers.
- Greet the students pleasantly and spend a few minutes in casual conversation before you actually begin work. As a rule, do not allow this conversation to exceed five minutes. Students will take their cue from you. If you encourage conversing rather than working, they will be more than willing to oblige.
- Participate fully in this pre-lesson conversation and listen attentively to the students' remarks. Often you can later refer to these remarks when you are helping students to understand a vocabulary word or a point in the reading selection. Not only do they appreciate the fact that you actually were listening to them, but also they begin to make connections with the material they are studying.
- Use a phrase such as "Shall we get started?" to indicate that it is time to begin the lesson. A consistent use of such transitional statements helps the students feel more comfortable with both you and the class routine.
- If possible, work at an uncluttered table rather than at desks. Try to have straight-backed, cushioned chairs since physical comfort makes developing a good relationship easier.
- Be sure to use positive reinforcement during the lesson. Remind students of the progress they are making. When a student is particularly discouraged, do this in a concrete way. For example, show him how many pages of work he has completed, or have him look at his composition book to see all the writing he has done.
- Develop the habit of wishing students a good day or a good evening as they leave the class. This is especially important if both you and the students have had a rough session. The students, particularly adolescents, need to know that you don't carry personal grudges.

Classroom Supplies

For each class, students need to bring their *Challenger* book, their composition book, and a pen or pencil. The use of the composition book—a slim, loose-leaf binder with wide-lined paper—is discussed in Chapter 5.

You need your own copy of *Challenger*, any notes and reinforcement activities pertaining to the lesson, a few sheets of blank paper for notes, and a pen. A pen is recommended because students can spot your marginal notes and corrections more easily. Avoid red ink as it is frequently associated with too many bad memories.

Have a dictionary and, if possible, a set of encyclopedias, a globe or an atlas within easy reach. The encyclopedia and the dictionary are valuable resources because they provide pictures and additional information about many of the words, people, and events mentioned in the reading selections and exercises. Be prepared to teach students how to use these resources. Do not assume that students working at a Book 5 reading level are familiar with them.

A globe or map is helpful because it can make the facts presented in the lessons more meaningful to students. For example, in Lesson 1, Exercise 1 of Book 5, students must match the Nile to the description "the longest river in Africa." This presents a good opportunity for students to locate the Nile on a globe or map.

Encourage students to research additional information as often as their interest, abilities, and time permit and give them all the assistance you can when they need help. These mini-research experiences help students feel more competent when searching for information.

A Summary of Do's

1. Do try to schedule at least two classes each week which meet at a regularly-appointed time.
2. Do take time to develop a consistent lesson format that will work well for your students.
3. Do perceive your students' work in terms of improvement rather than mastery.
4. Do take time to prepare for each class.
5. Do give yourself a few moments to relax before each class.
6. Do develop a good working relationship with students because it is essential to their reading progress.
7. Do make sure that the environment in which you teach is as conducive to good learning as possible.
8. Do have reference and resource materials available, if possible.
9. Do give the students positive reinforcement during the lessons.

3. Teaching the Lessons

In this chapter, suggestions are given for teaching the main components of each lesson. These components include word study, the reading selection, the exercises, correcting the homework, and the homework preview.

Word Study

The *Challenger* series places a great deal of emphasis on learning and/or reviewing word meanings since a major obstacle to reading development is a poor vocabulary. It has been estimated that only about 2,000 words account for 99% of everything we say. To be a proficient reader, however, one must be familiar with far more than 2,000 words. Thus, except for the reading comprehension exercises, most of the other exercises focus on vocabulary development.

Word Charts and Definitions

As mentioned previously, the word charts contain new words that are organized around common phonics principles. Most of these principles have been introduced in earlier books and are being reviewed in Book 5. How much emphasis you give to the phonics principles depends upon the needs of your students. Some students enjoy reading the chart words aloud, while others prefer to start each class with the definitions exercise. Words from the chart are repeated frequently in Book 5 exercises, so it is not essential that students read the chart words aloud. For those who do, however, emphasize pronunciation only. Meanings are stressed in the definitions exercise and in many other exercises.

Words for Study

Keep in mind that the *Challenger* series is a controlled vocabulary series. When students wish to know how the words listed in the Words for Study at the beginning of each lesson have been selected, inform them that these words are appearing for the first time in the series. Most of the other words in each lesson have appeared earlier in the series.

Students not only find the concept of a controlled vocabulary interesting, but some interpret this concept in interesting ways. For example, one student who was experiencing difficulty with a synonym exercise in Book 6 remarked: "Well, you can't expect me to know words that were studied in Book 5!"

Behind this statement is a conviction shared by many reading students that once you've studied a word, you should never have to study it again. Unfortunately, this is not true. Words are learned through repetition, practice, and using the dictionary. Do not assume that your students know this. Simply remind them, when appropriate, that a good reading vocabulary is necessary for

good reading and that they will encounter a word in various types of exercises so that they can truly master its meaning.

The best way to encourage your students as they complete the many vocabulary development exercises is to demonstrate an interest in language yourself. This does not mean that you have to use a lot of "fancy" words when talking to your students. What it does mean is that you do not approach vocabulary study as if it were something merely to be endured.

Suggestions for Enriching Word Study

Here are a few suggestions for making vocabulary study more interesting for students:

1. Have students pronounce the Words for Study in the next lesson during the homework preview. Most words will not give them any trouble. By pronouncing the unfamiliar ones, students will gain confidence in their ability to learn the word, and confidence often leads to interest.

2. Encourage students to develop the habit of paying attention to word endings. Words listed in the Words for Study appear in the same form in which they appear in the reading. For example, notice that in Lesson 1, *following* is listed. Emphasis on accurate pronunciations of endings will help students with both their reading and writing.

3. When time permits, spend a few minutes in casual conversation about some of the words. Using the Words for Study in Lesson 2 as an example, you may wish to talk about the different ways the word *grant* can be used, or have students identify the root in *reaction*, or help them to trace the origin of *synonym* in a good dictionary. Occasional discussion of words helps students to see them as more than just a string of letters.

4. Take time during discussions of the readings to highlight vocabulary and/or language features. In Lesson 2, students enjoy substituting more colloquial language for the formal speech of King Midas and Bacchus. These brief activities help students to see that language patterns vary from group to group and that language is always changing.

5. Finally, strive to speak with expression. You needn't be a Broadway star, but a little ham goes a long way.

The Reading Selections

The amount of time you allot to oral reading and discussion of the reading selections ultimately depends on both the needs of your students and how much class time you have with them.

Pre-reading and Post-reading Activities

Students working in Book 5 need to develop strategies for increasing their literal, interpretive, and critical comprehension skills. There are many types of pre-reading and post-reading activities to aid them in this process.

Pre-reading activities should accomplish one or more of the following objectives:

1. to stimulate students' interest by drawing on their prior experience and understanding of the subject.
2. to provide essential background information.
3. to give students a purpose for reading.

You can link the subject of the reading to students' own experiences by asking "Have you ever done/been/thought/felt ...?" questions. Some of the readings are better understood if the historical setting is first discussed or described. It is also helpful to set a task for students as they read. For example, for the story in Lesson 1 you might say, "As you read, think about what kind of person Grandpa was."

Read the first few paragraphs of each reading selection aloud to the students. Have them follow along in the book as you read. Then ask one or two questions to make sure students have understood what you read. By reading aloud, you can create interest in the reading and give students a feel for the author's style and tone. At the same time, you are modelling good reading for your students.

After students have finished reading the selection for homework, have a general discussion to refresh their memories and to make sure they have understood the reading. Then discuss their responses to any pre-reading task you set for them. Also discuss their responses to the comprehension exercises.

You should make a list of pre- and post-reading questions and/or activities for each reading selection based on your students' backgrounds, capabilities, and needs. The individual lesson notes give some suggestions.

Encourage students to talk about how they feel about the readings. Remember that literature evokes emotional as well as intellectual responses and is meant to be enjoyable.

Oral Reading

Having students read aloud at least part of the reading selection periodically gives you an opportunity to note their strengths and weaknesses and also to help them develop good oral reading habits. Some students are under the impression that good oral reading means that one reads as fast as one can. Remind these students that in oral reading one must always be conscious of the needs of the listeners.

Discussing the Reading

To create an atmosphere in which the reading selections and student thoughts about them can be discussed with a sense of harmony and unity, consider these suggestions.

1. Plan questions that you want to ask in class. Be prepared, however, to put your planned questions aside when a spontaneous question arises in class.
2. Make sure students understand the basic ground rule of all good discussions: one person speaks at a time.
3. Encourage participation, but don't force it. Likewise, discourage students from monopolizing the discussion.
4. Keep the discussion focused.
5. Avoid asking "yes" and "no" questions. Discussions, like travel, should be broadening. "Yes" and "no" questions shut off discussion by being answerable in a single word. They also imply that the student should have reached a conclusion before the discussion has even started.
6. If students seem confused by your questions, rephrase them rather than repeating them word-for-word. This practice is not only courteous, but it also reminds students that there is usually more than one way to phrase an idea.

These suggestions represent the easier part of moderating a discussion. The harder part is staying out of the way. Your task as the moderator is to get students to react to each other's opinions and comments, not to dominate the discussion yourself.

It is essential to view discussions in the same way that you view the students' other work—in terms of improvement, or growth, instead of mastery. It takes time to develop a good discussion group in which participants can learn to really listen to each other and gain confidence to express themselves as genuinely as possible. Do not expect it to be otherwise.

Through these discussions, students begin to sense a relationship between the lesson material and their own lives. The relationships they have with you and the other students can become more relaxed and real. This, in turn, means that everyone learns better and faster.

The Exercises

In the exercises, students develop their reasoning abilities because they are required to think and infer, to use context clues, to practice the process of elimination, and to apply what they already know to new situations.

Three points that you should emphasize to students are accuracy, legibility, and completeness. They are to spell their responses correctly and legibly, and they are not to leave any item blank. Tell them to answer all questions to the best of their ability. Not only does learning thrive on corrected mistakes, but also much is to be said for the art of intelligent guessing.

Remind students to check over their homework after they have finished all the exercises to make sure they have answered all questions completely and accurately.

Allow enough time at the end of the class period for previewing the exercises that are to be completed for homework. It is important that students understand exactly what is expected of them, so don't rush this segment of the lesson.

You should spend a few minutes during the first class meeting with your students to review the importance of homework. Remember, some of your students haven't been in a school situation for quite a while, and they may need to be reminded of the importance of completing the assignments as well as they can.

Sometimes students try to complete the homework right after a full day's (or full night's) work, or just before going to bed, or while they are trying to fulfill other responsibilities. Suggest that they schedule a definite, 30-minute study time in quiet surroundings when they are not exhausted.

Make sure to present your ideas on how to develop better study habits in the form of suggestions. You are not stating policy; you are simply encouraging students to think about how they can better achieve their reading goals within the circumstances of their lives.

Correcting the Homework

Be sure you allow enough time to go over the homework with the students. You will probably need to observe your students and try out a few different schedules before you hit on the pace that works best for them. But once you establish the appropriate pace, consistency promotes good concentration and effective learning.

Of all the lesson segments—the words for study, the reading selection, and the exercises—the exercises should be covered most thoroughly. All the homework should be corrected. Remember that many patterns are being established. If students develop the habit of doing something incorrectly, they will have a hard time un-learning the procedure. Be sure to explain this to the students. Eventually, they adapt to this procedure because they see that the more they correct in the early stages, the less they have to correct later.

Too often, going over the homework can be nothing more than a dry, mechanical routine in which students simply read their answers. Not only does this deprive them of practice with the words and concepts they've been studying, but also it is unfair. Consciously or unconsciously, the students' efforts are being slighted if the homework critique is being done in a dreary, "what's-the-answer-to-number-2?" style.

Take your time and enjoy this part of the lesson. If opportunities arise for brief tangents in which items are related to life experiences or other bits of information, take advantage of them.

Above all, don't forget to express your appreciation for students' efforts. Your supportive remarks should be brief and spoken in a natural voice. Excessive praise is ultimately as counterproductive as no praise at all. Words of encouragement should stress the notion of progress because students are progressing as they complete each lesson.

The Homework Preview

During the homework preview the students note what to do in the next lesson, which they are to complete for homework. Begin by going over the words listed in the Words for Study. Then introduce the reading selection to give students an idea of what they will be reading about. It may be necessary to help students get into the habit of noting the title of the reading selection. They should understand that the title gives them a general idea of what the selection is about and helps to focus their attention.

Remind students to refer to the reading selection when they cannot recall an answer to a comprehension question. In many instances, they may need to make intelligent guesses based on information which is implied rather than stated directly.

At this point in their reading development, all students are able to skim through the exercises and ask questions about words and/or directions with no assistance from you. The individual lesson notes indicate those instances in which you may want to emphasize certain words or directions.

A Summary of Do's

1. Do take time when necessary to explain to students how vocabulary study, the reading selections, and exercises contribute to their reading development.

2. Do make vocabulary study as interesting as possible.

3. Do plan pre-reading and post-reading activities to develop students' literal, interpretive, and critical comprehension skills.

4. Do encourage students to have an attitude of growth rather than fixed opinions in their discussions.

5. Do remind students, when necessary, of the significant role that homework plays in reading development.

6. Do emphasize the need for thoroughness, correct spelling, and accuracy in completing each exercise.

7. Do strive for completeness and enthusiasm in the homework reviews.

8. Do support the students' progress by taking the time to point out growth they have demonstrated in their work.

9. Do allow enough time at the end of each lesson to go over the Words for Study, introduce the next reading selection, and preview the homework exercises.

4. Reinforcement Activities

As the term suggests, these activities are designed to reinforce the students' understanding and retention of the lesson material. All students and most teachers occasionally need a break in the routine. Reinforcement activities may throw your schedule off a bit, but it's worth it. Just make sure that you leave enough time at the end of the class period to preview the homework.

At this point in students' development, two types of activities are particularly helpful:
- Activities which reinforce vocabulary skills.
- Occasional, short exercises which focus on mechanical or usage errors most of your students repeatedly make in their compositions.

The types of activities you use and the frequency with which you use them depend on the needs of your students and how often you have an opportunity to meet with them. The suggestions in this section are based on activities that students have found both helpful and enjoyable. This list is by no means complete. Take some time to develop your own "bag of tricks." Through talking with other teachers, skimming puzzle magazines, and using your own imagination, you will soon have reinforcement activities for a variety of skills. Students, too, often recall helpful activities from their earlier schooling. In fact, some of the suggestions which follow come from students.

Word and Information Games

Students working at this level often enjoy games that are modeled after television shows such as *Jeopardy*. These activities take some time to prepare, but they are an excellent way to reinforce vocabulary and information presented in the lessons. Certainly you can prepare the questions, but having the students do it gives them an excellent opportunity to review the material.

Students can create their own *Jeopardy* games by preparing sets of questions based on the reading selections. They can also create sets of vocabulary questions. For example, all the answers in a category might begin with the prefix *pre-* or the letter *s*. Other appropriate categories include: State Capitals, Bodies of Water, U.S. Presidents, Roman Gods and Goddesses, Famous Inventors, Abbreviations, and so on.

Other game show formats can also be used. For example, students enjoy playing their own version of *Wheel of Fortune*. They also enjoy their version of *College Bowl* in which two teams compete against each other. In this game, the teacher can prepare the questions and act as the moderator.

Puzzles

Many puzzles and other activities can be found in puzzle magazines sold in most drugstores and supermarkets. You can create your own puzzles using these formats and vocabulary from past and current word indexes. The word indexes for Book 5 are at the back of this manual. If you have access to a computer, there is software available for creating crossword puzzles into which you can insert vocabulary words to be reinforced.

Spelling Bees or Drills

This activity is most helpful when a specific principle is emphasized; for example, selecting words which all contain a specific suffix or consonant blend, or which belong to the same word family. Again, the word indexes at the back of this manual can be helpful in developing these activities. Drills should be spontaneous, brief—10 words is usually sufficient—and informally presented. In other words, they should not resemble a quiz in which students demonstrate mastery. Rather they are an opportunity to help students to better understand certain language principles that are giving them difficulty.

Worksheets

One type of worksheet can focus on some principle that is giving students trouble, such as recognizing analogies, using context clues, or making inferences. A popular type of worksheet for context clue or vocabulary reinforcement is to collect sentences from a newspaper or magazine in which troublesome words you have been working with appear. Set them up in a fill-in-the-blank format for the students to complete as a group. As one student once remarked, "You mean people actually do use these words?" You might also tell students to be on the lookout for these words and have them bring to class examples that they find in their own reading.

Another type of worksheet can give students practice with some aspect of writing, such as capitalization or punctuation. For example, many students neglect to use commas after introductory clauses. You might prepare ten sentences which begin with introductory clauses and have the students insert commas appropriately. Students find this type of introduction to grammar both tolerable and beneficial because it helps them to recall a rule they need for their own writing.

Enrichment Projects

Students can spend some time in the library seeking additional information about people or topics presented in the lessons and informally report their findings to the class. These reports can be given during the time set aside for reinforcement activities.

Any additional information that you can present also heightens the students' interest in the material. For example, for Lesson 2, you might have copies of easy-to-read collections of myths available so that students can read other myths related to Bacchus or to some of the other gods. You might bring to class photos of statues of the gods or of some of the many paintings that depict the ancient myths. Students could collect references to the gods that they find in newspapers and magazines. The individual lesson notes contain some suggestions for enrichment ideas.

Activities Based on Student Needs

Occasionally students may have specific personal needs, such as filling out an application form or creating a resume, that can be fit comfortably into the lesson format as reinforcement activities if they tell you about them far enough in advance. However, reinforcement activities are to reinforce, not replace, the lessons. If students are spending most of their valuable class time hearing additional information about the reading selections or getting your assistance with personal needs, they may learn some interesting facts or get forms filled out, but they are not progressing in their reading development.

If you suspect that students are using reinforcement activities to avoid working on the lessons, you probably need to help them clarify their learning goals. Gently but firmly remind them that, in the long run, their reading and writing will progress more rapidly if they concentrate more on the lesson work and recognize that the primary reason for reinforcement activities is to do just that—reinforce.

A Note to the Teacher

Because it takes time to prepare many of these reinforcement activities, be sure to file them away for use with future students.

Also, do not pressure yourself to come up with something new every time you plan a reinforcement activity. It takes a few years to develop a solid file of activities.

A Summary of Do's and Don'ts

1. Do make sure the scheduled lesson time is not sacrificed for reinforcement activities.
2. Do involve the students in planning and creating reinforcement activities whenever possible.
3. Do plan and implement activities that address both the students' learning needs and their personal needs.
4. Do remember to save materials you develop for future use.
5. Don't foster a "here's-some-more-hard-work" attitude toward reinforcement activities. The students have just finished discussing a reading selection, reviewing their homework, and learning new material. If the reinforcement activities are to benefit them, they need a little more informality from you for this segment of the lesson.
6. Don't foster a "this-is-just-for-fun" attitude either. Students might not find the activities enjoyable. And you want students who do find them enjoyable to recognize that pleasure and learning can go hand in hand.

5. Writing

Because the major purpose of this reading series is to help students develop their reading skills, less emphasis has been placed on writing skills. Even though writing is an important skill, it is a distinct skill that requires a great deal of practice and instruction time. Generally, the writing activities included in Book 5 focus on clarity and completeness of expression, coherence of thought, basic grammar, and spelling. However, there are plentiful opportunities for students to express their own opinions and ideas in writing.

Why Writing Is Included

The teacher can assume that a student who has completed some of the books which precede Book 5 can write complete sentences and coherent paragraphs. These students will not be surprised at the exercises which involve writing in the later *Challenger* books.

Students who are new to this series may wonder why writing activities have been included in a reading series. When this is the case, take time to point out the following:

- Writing is part of literacy. To be literate, a person must be able to write as well as read.
- Writing helps students to formulate and express their thoughts more precisely. This type of thinking helps them to complete the other exercises more rapidly.
- The writing that students do in these lessons will help them with other types of writing they may want to do, such as letters, reports, and short paragraphs on job applications or resumes.
- Only through actually writing can students see that they are able to write.

Opportunities for Writing

In Book 5, primary emphasis is placed on content, rather than on the mechanics of writing. The reading comprehension questions require students to draw conclusions from inferences, to cite reasons to support their opinions, to give explanations for their answers, and to cite examples and details to support their responses. There are also opportunities for imaginative writing, such as predicting the endings to stories.

The individual lesson notes include many suggestions for writing assignments which can supplement the lessons as reinforcement activities. As stated in Chapter 1, it is recommended that weekly writing assignments of 100-125 words be given. However, the decision on how often to give writing assignments as homework should depend on the teacher's assessment of the students' time, personal needs, and capabilities. The key word is flexibility.

How to Handle Writing Assignments

When students have been given a writing assignment, have them share their work at the beginning of the next class session. Working in pairs or small groups, students can read their assignments aloud to one another and react to each other's writing on the basis of content and organization. Students can then exchange papers and act as editors or proofreaders, checking for mechanical problems such as missing words, spelling, capitalization, and punctuation. Give students the opportunity to revise their assignments before collecting them at the following class session.

When responding to these writing assignments, try to make positive comments as well as noting areas for improvement. Your reactions should be based more on the content, style, and organization of the writing than on the mechanical aspects.

It is recommended that students keep all writing assignments in a slim, loose-leaf binder with wide-lined notebook paper. Composition books enable both the students and the teacher to quickly review student progress. Have them date their work. As the weeks and months progress, most students enjoy looking back now and then at all the writing they have done and how much they have accomplished.

Like reading and vocabulary work, writing must be seen in terms of improvement rather than mastery. Most students read far better than they write. It is not uncommon for a student working in Book 6, for example, to write at a Book 4 level: very simple sentences, few modifiers, and underdeveloped thoughts. The most common reason for this is lack of practice. Allow students to develop from their own starting points, making them aware of their strengths as well as helping them to work on their weaknesses. And don't forget to be patient.

Here are a few suggestions to consider in helping students with their writing:

- As often as possible, have students read their written responses or compositions aloud. Students usually enjoy doing this, and it gives them a chance to hear whether or not their writing makes sense. Insist on honest but courteously presented reactions from the other students.
- Occasionally, allot some class time to studying how the professional writers write. Use a reading selection from *Challenger* or an interesting magazine article. Help students analyze the piece of writing on the basis of content organization and style. Make sure students understand that the writing they are analyzing is more than a second, third, or fourth draft. Few students recognize the contribution editing makes in the writing

process, and understanding this makes them feel less discouraged about their writing difficulties.

- With their permission, use writing from previous or present students as models to explain a particularly difficult writing assignment. Seeing the work of their peers often helps students realize that the teacher is not asking them to do the impossible.

- With their permission, compile a worksheet using sentences from student work which illustrate common mistakes. For example, a worksheet comprised of student-created run-on sentences is an excellent reinforcement activity. Students can work together in class to correct the errors and better understand how to avoid this particular writing problem.

- Provide the opportunity for students to publicly display their final drafts so other students can read them.

Dealing with Typical Writing Problems
Run-on Sentences

This situation demands consummate tact on your part because, invariably, the student thinks he has written a terrific sentence and is dismayed to learn that he has to divide it into three or four shorter sentences. Help him to see that, by using commas and periods wherever necessary, he helps readers to follow his thoughts more easily. To illustrate how punctuation helps the reader, have him read the sentence aloud, telling him to pause only at commas and to take a breath only at a period. If you prefer, you can demonstrate by reading his sentence to him. When he recognizes the value of punctuation marks, have him revise the run-on sentence as necessary. Be sure to commend him for his effort in helping to make his writing easier for readers to comprehend.

Omitted Words

When reading their sentences aloud, students are often surprised to see that they have omitted words. Remind them that many writers have this problem because the mind can think faster than the hand can write. Suggest that after they have written something, they should read it to themselves, pointing to each word as they encounter it. This strategy will help them learn to monitor their writing.

Confusing Sentences

When a student writes a sentence which is confusing, tell him you don't understand what he's trying to express and ask him to explain what he meant. Once you understand his intent, start a more coherent version of his sentence and have him finish it. After the student has read the revision, ask him if it matches what he meant. If not, work on the sentence until the revision accurately expresses the student's original idea.

Problems with Content and Organization

Students often have difficulty finding enough to say in their writing assignments and organizing their thoughts in a logical or interesting manner. Suggest that they begin by making notes of everything they can think of pertaining to the topic. The next step is to select from their notes the specific points and details that they want to include in their composition. Then they should organize those points and details in the order in which they want to include them. They should do all of this *before* writing their first draft. After the first draft is written, they should read it to see if they want to add anything more or to rearrange any of the points.

A Summary of Do's and Don'ts

1. Do tailor writing assignments to meet the students' needs and capabilities.
2. Do make sure that students understand the purpose and value of writing practice.
3. Do have students keep an orderly composition book for all their writing.
4. Do make sure that written work is evaluated, and when appropriate, have students write at least a second draft.
5. Do provide opportunities for students to share their writing with each other.
6. Don't expect the students' writing levels to be as high as their reading levels.
7. Don't allow writing assignments to become more important than the lessons and other necessary reinforcement activities.

6. Using the Lesson Notes

Because you are already familiar with the principles and procedures that pertain to the lessons in general from reading the previous chapters in this manual, you have the necessary foundation for sound instructional practices. The lesson notes address some specific points for the individual lessons. As part of class preparation, you should review the notes for the lesson assigned for homework. You should also read the notes for the lesson which you will be previewing to decide on how best to introduce the reading and to note any suggestions and reminders that might be helpful to the students when they are doing their homework.

Keep in mind that the lesson notes are only suggestions based on the experience of other reading teachers. If you try one of the suggestions a few times and find it doesn't work, disregard it.

Items of Primary and Secondary Emphasis

In most cases, the items listed under the "Primary emphasis" heading deal with comprehension of literature and vocabulary development. Using context clues and using the dictionary receive primary emphasis, also. The first time a particular task is introduced as an exercise, it also is listed under "Primary emphasis."

Items listed under "Secondary emphasis" receive less emphasis in the lesson. Many are skills which have been introduced previously and are now being reinforced.

The Reading Selection

The lesson notes contain suggestions for introducing the reading selections and for discussing them. The reading segment of the lesson demands more flexibility on the teacher's part than any other. Students vary greatly in ability and motivation. Remember that the key to helping students make the greatest gains in the least amount of time is observation. Carefully monitoring your students' progress will help you to develop sound procedures for improving reading and comprehension skills.

Developing Your Own Notes

Develop the habit of keeping your own notes. Take time at the end of each class session to write down any remarks or reminders about particular difficulties students may have had with the lesson. Also make note of specific words or skills for which you may want to develop reinforcement activities.

Be sure to also keep notes of any procedures and techniques which seem to work well. Often you will hit upon an excellent way to present a certain skill or concept. Take some time to jot down your idea, especially if you know that you won't have the opportunity to use it again until a much later time. So much patience and concentration is called for in teaching reading that it's easy to forget those great ideas.

7. Lesson Notes for Book 5

Lesson 1
Review of Long and Short Vowels

Primary emphasis

- Comprehension (written questions and answers)
- Using the dictionary
- Using context clues

Secondary emphasis

- Vocabulary review (Which Word Does Not Fit?)
- Compound words
- Oral reading

Word Chart

As was mentioned in the introduction to Book 5, the Word Chart presents a systematic form through which the student is introduced to new words in this reading series. How much emphasis the teacher places upon the Word Chart as a review of phonics concepts should depend exclusively on the needs of the student.

Generally, the student who has started his reading work in either Book 1 or Book 2 benefits from pronouncing the words which appear on the chart for each lesson. These students still depend on phonics rules to help them sound out new words.

All other students usually enjoy reading the words, but it is not necessary that they do so. Thus, if you find that time can be more beneficially spent on another part of the lesson or appropriate reinforcement activity, the phonics principle which underscores each Word Chart can be mentioned in passing rather than emphasized as a learning activity, and the reading of the words on the chart can be omitted.

Do not dwell on the definitions when doing any word chart work because students encounter troublesome words in the first exercise for all lessons and in exercises in subsequent lessons of the book. The teacher is to make a mental note of those words which give the student continued difficulty and incorporate them in future reinforcement activities.

Exercise 1: Word Meanings

For this exercise, students should use a dictionary to look up unfamiliar words. Students should be expected to complete these exercises with 100% accuracy. If a student consistently makes two or more mistakes on word meaning exercises, spend some time helping him to pinpoint the reasons for his errors. Always encourage students to learn from their mistakes rather than to see them as signs of failure.

A major reason that students complain about having to learn definitions is that they do not understand the significance of vocabulary work. Make sure students understand that knowing the meanings of words is vital to reading comprehension.

In all exercises in which copying is involved, students should copy accurately. They should correct any words they miscopy. When this expectation of accuracy is gently but consistently encouraged, the students themselves will begin to adopt a standard of accuracy and demonstrate more patience and pride in the quality of their work.

Story

The Words for Study section contains words that appear in this lesson for the first time in this controlled-vocabulary reading series.

Tell students that the reading selections appearing in this book are adapted from well-known, critically acclaimed works. It motivates students to know that they are reading widely respected material. Introduce or review the terms *fiction* and *nonfiction*.

Generally, students should read the selections for homework, but because this is the first lesson, allot time for an oral first reading in class. Introduce the story by asking students if there are stories about family members that their families enjoy telling. Point out the title and ask what students think the story will be about. Read the first paragraph of the story aloud. Ask students if they think this story will be serious or humorous. Discuss the humorous tone of the phrase "when brains were passed out he must have been somewhere else." Continue reading this first story aloud. Stop occasionally to ask a question, if you think it is necessary. Don't stop too often to ask questions, however, as this can be disruptive to comprehension and enjoyment.

After reading the story aloud, discuss it in a general way. This gives students a chance to get a sense of the story as a whole while giving you the opportunity to assess their comprehension skills. Begin the discussion by asking such questions as: "Did you like this story? Why or why not?," "What kind of person was Grandpa?," and "How do you think the author felt about Grandpa?"

When you have completed the general discussion of the story, preview the exercises to be done for homework. Since this is the first lesson, take plenty of time and be sure all students understand how to do each exercise. If necessary, have students complete an item in each exercise during the preview so that they have a thorough understanding of how to do the work. Discuss the importance of homework and compare it to the daily practice that sports and music require.

Exercise 2: About the Story

During the homework preview, tell students to refer to the story when necessary in answering the questions, rather than to guess or to leave an answer blank. Students should complete *all* the questions for all exercises.

For students who wish to know why they cannot simply put the letter of the correct answer on the line, remind them that any opportunity to write out a word is good spelling practice.

If a student has trouble answering a multiple choice question, encourage him to refer back to the reading selection. Students can also eliminate the obviously incorrect answers and then evaluate the remaining choices to select the correct one.

An appropriate follow-up composition would be to have students describe a humorous incident involving themselves, a relative, or a friend, or to write about their favorite relative.

Exercise 3: Which Word Does Not Fit?

Students who have worked in the earlier books in this series are familiar with this type of exercise. If you have students who are starting in Book 5, have them read the directions and complete the first two items during the homework preview so that they fully understand what is expected of them.

Exercise 4: Grandpa Celebrates His Good Luck

Review the definition for *compound word* with all students. Again, students who have worked in the earlier books are quite familiar with this type of exercise. For the student who is starting in Book 5, have him read the directions, study the example, and complete one item during the homework preview so that he fully understands what is expected of him.

Remind students to work by process of elimination and to look for clues in the sentences themselves to help them find the right answers. It is not necessary that the student complete the items of this or any other exercise in order; it is perfectly all right to skip around. However, remind the student to check his work after having completed an exercise. Skipping around sometimes leads to skipping items.

Note

After the student has gone over the exercises and made any necessary corrections during the homework review, give him an opportunity to ask questions or make comments about what he has just accomplished. If he seems overwhelmed by the work, point out the strengths he has shown in completing the work. Remind him that this is only the first lesson and that he will get used to the work more quickly than he thinks is possible.

Lesson 2
Review of Consonant Blends and Digraphs: Part 1

Primary emphasis
- Comprehension (written questions and answers)
- Using the dictionary
- Using context clues

Secondary emphasis
- Vocabulary review (synonyms)
- Review of consonant blends (*ch, sh, st*)
- Oral reading

Word Chart and Word Meanings

Use the procedure suggested for Lesson 1.

Words for Study

1. Make sure the student can pronounce *Midas* and *Bacchus*.
2. Save your explanation of the word *synonym* for the preview of Exercise 4. All students are encountering this word for the first time in this reading series.

Story

During the preview, introduce this reading by telling students that it is a well-known myth. Explain that the main characters in myths are usually gods and heroes. The Greeks and Romans had many myths that are still familiar to us today.

Point out the title and ask students what they think the story will be about. Explain that the two main characters are Bacchus, the god of wine, and King Midas. Ask if anyone knows the story of King Midas. If a student is familiar with this myth, have him summarize it for the class.

In the discussion during the homework review, ask students if they know any other stories about Greek or Roman gods. You might point out that the other planets in our solar system are named after Greek or Roman gods. If students are interested in reading more myths, the public library has many books containing versions of Greek and Roman myths.

Exercise 2: About the Story

For item 5, students appreciate it if you allow them to write the correct letter before each cause and then write out the causes after any necessary corrections have been made during the homework review. Item 6 provides a good starting point for a brief class discussion or a longer composition.

Exercise 3: Strange Sentences

Many students find it helpful if you remind them to initially read each sentence in its entirety prior to filling in the blanks. For example, sentence 1 should be read, "*Blank* first *blank* for dessert was a piece of *blank blank*, but then he *blank* his mind.*" If necessary, remind the student to use process of elimination to complete this exercise.

Exercise 4: Working with Synonyms

Make sure the student can correctly pronounce and verbalize the definition for *synonym* during the homework preview. Have him complete the second item so that he has a clear understanding of how this exercise is to be completed. Students often ask if they can use the dictionary for this exercise. Needless to say, the answer is "YES!"

Oral Reading

Note that oral reading is listed as an objective in this and all subsequent lessons. Try to have either the entire story, part of the story, and/or the exercises read aloud as often as time permits. When necessary, help the student to develop good oral reading habits. Some students are under the impression that good oral reading means that one reads as fast as he can. In these instances, remind the student that, in oral reading, one must always be conscious of the needs of the listeners.

Adolescents enjoy the opportunity to practice reading aloud, and adults appreciate it. Many adult students have wanted to read to their children, but have been fearful of doing so. This practice helps them to increase both their ability and confidence.

Lesson 3
Review of Consonant Blends: Part 2

Primary emphasis

- Comprehension (written questions and answers)
- Using the dictionary
- Using context clues

Secondary emphasis

- Vocabulary review (synonyms; analogies)
- Review of consonant blends (*bl, br, cl, cr, fl, fr*)
- Oral reading

Word Chart and Word Meanings

Use the procedure suggested for Lesson 1.

Words for Study

Make sure the student understands the meaning of *panhandled* during the homework preview. The meaning of this word cannot be clearly discerned from the story. In most instances, the student should attempt to learn the meanings of confusing words from the stories and/or exercises in which they appear. Words such as *panhandled*, which are discussed during the preview, are the exception rather than the rule.

Story

Introduce this story by asking students what they think the title means. Ask "Can you think of any time when what you were wearing influenced how you behaved or how people behaved toward you?" Tell students this story is set in Paris and have them find Paris on a world map or globe. Explain that a character in this story undergoes an abrupt change. Tell students that as they read the story they should try to predict what will happen.

Students may need to read this story more than once to comprehend the subtleties. Many inferences have to be made to understand the plot and to see the humor in it. Discuss the plot with students to be sure they know what took place in the story.

In the discussion during the homework review, ask: "How would you describe Tango at the beginning of the story?" Discuss how the author reveals Tango's character through the opening dialogue and actions. Have students cite lines from the story to support their descriptions.

As a follow-up writing or discussion topic, have students tell how Tango changes in this story and what causes the transformation.

Exercise 2: About the Story

Students' interpretation of some of these questions may vary. Accept any answer the student can justify in the context of the story. Discuss the fact that different readers will interpret a work of fiction differently because they have different backgrounds and experiences which they bring to the interpretation.

Encourage students to use the dictionary to find the answers to questions 9 and 10 if necessary.

When going over the answers during the homework review, make sure that students have used complete sentences to answer the "What do you think?" question. Initially, students may have difficulty putting their answers in sentence form, but with practice they will become increasingly proficient.

Exercise 3: More Strange Sentences

If necessary, remind the student of the appropriate procedure to use to complete this exercise.

Exercise 4: Synonyms

Review the meaning of *synonym* during the preview.

Exercise 5: Which Word Fits Best?

Students often have difficulty with this type of exercise. Help students get started by completing the first question during the preview. Ask them to explain the relationship between *cleat* and *football*. Then have them read the four choices and decide which word expresses a similar relationship to *mouthpiece*. Most students will see that *boxing* is the sport in which a *mouthpiece* is used.

Students enjoy hearing that this type of question is on the College Entrance Examination. Whether or not you choose to introduce the term *analogy* is up to you—some students are impressed by the sound of this word.

Lesson 4
Review of Consonant Blends: Part 3

Primary emphasis

- Comprehension (written questions and answers)
- Using the dictionary
- Using context clues

Secondary emphasis

- Vocabulary review (antonyms)
- Compound words
- Review of consonant blends (*gl, gr, pl, pr, sl, str*)
- Oral reading

Word Chart and Word Meanings

Use the procedure suggested for Lesson 1.

Words for Study

Save your explanation of *antonym* for the preview of Exercise 4. All students are encountering this word for the first time in this reading series.

Story

During the preview, introduce this story by telling students that O. Henry is a well-known author who is famous for his surprise endings. Tell them to watch for clues to the ending as they read the story. In the discussion during the homework review, ask students to point out clues that foreshadow the ending, such as the man's scar, his expensive watch, the fact that "Jimmy" was taller, and so forth. Discuss foreshadowing as a device writers use to prepare the reader for what will come later.

In a follow-up composition, students might write about what they expect to be doing 20 years from now.

Exercise 2: About the Story

During the preview, have students read the directions and study the example carefully to be sure they understand how to do this exercise. If necessary, have them complete the next one or two items in class also.

The Answer Key provides suggested revisions for the false statements. Some statements can be corrected in more than one way. Accept any correct revision.

Exercise 3: Working with Antonyms

Make sure the student can correctly pronounce and verbalize the definition for *antonym* during the homework preview. Have him complete the second item so that he has a clear understanding of how this exercise is to be completed.

If necessary, remind him to work by process of elimination.

Exercise 4: Strange Verses

During the homework review, consider using this exercise for oral reading practice. Students may need help in reading the verses with appropriate rhythm.

Exercise 5: Compound Words

The student is to use the same procedure he used to complete this type of exercise in Lesson 1.

Review: Lessons 1-4

As was the case in the earlier books, it should be emphasized to the student that this is a review, not a test. Material is often presented in new ways to both challenge the student and, hopefully, arouse his interest.

Preview each exercise included in the review as you would a lesson. If appropriate, have the student complete an item in each exercise during the preview so that he has a better understanding of how to do the work.

An overall score of 80% or better on a review exercise should be considered excellent.

These reviews appear after every four lessons. The word indexes, which include the words that have been introduced in Book 5 to date, can be used as the basis for reinforcement activities such as spelling quizzes, vocabulary reviews, and word games.

Exercise 6: Helping People

If students are encountering this type of puzzle for the first time, have them complete a few of the items during the homework preview. Have them fill in the appropriate blanks in the quotation as they answer each item. In this way, they can work back and forth between the clues and the quotation, using context clues in the quotation to complete the partially filled-in words.

Lesson 5
Review of Consonant Blends: Part 4

Primary emphasis

- Comprehension (written questions and answers)
- Using the dictionary
- Using context clues

Secondary emphasis

- Vocabulary review
- Syllabication
- Review of consonant blends
- Oral reading

Word Chart and Word Meanings

Use the procedure suggested for Lesson 1.

Story

During the preview, point out that this story is in two parts. Students will be reading only the first part for this lesson. Draw students' attention to the title and ask them what they think the story might be about. Have them describe some tricks that have been played on them. During the review, ask students to describe George's character. What clues to his character can they find in the text? Discuss students' ideas about how they would end the story.

Exercise 3: Working with Consonant Blends and Digraphs

During the preview, suggest that students use context clues to figure out words that make sense in each sentence. Then they should check the list of blends to make sure that the blends they selected are included. You may want to do the first sentence together as a group to be sure students understand what is expected of them.

Exercise 4: Which Word Does Not Fit?

If necessary, have the student complete an item during the homework preview. Most students have little difficulty with this exercise.

Exercise 5: Breaking Words into Syllables

Review the definition of *syllable*. Students who have worked in earlier books have virtually no difficulty with this exercise. For the student who has started in Book 5, it may be necessary to have him complete a few items during the homework preview. If a student asks you if he can refer to the dictionary for the correct answers, tell him that you want to see how well he can do on this exercise without the aid of the dictionary. In this way, you have an opportunity to learn what the student knows about syllabication.

Because using the dictionary is a primary objective for all lessons in Book 5, the student may use this resource for any subsequent exercise pertaining to syllabication.

If the student does demonstrate some difficulty completing this exercise, plan some syllabication work as a reinforcement activity on an occasional basis. Make sure that the student understands that this type of activity contributes to overall spelling improvement.

Exercise 6: Where Can You Find It?

Some students need to be reminded that each word in the left column is to be used only once. Thus, *stench*, which is an appropriate answer for *battle*, must be matched with *trash can* in order to match *bloodshed* correctly. (Some students insist that *stench* should be matched with *sneakers*.)

Lesson 6
Review of Consonant Blends: Part 5

Primary emphasis

- Comprehension (written questions and answers)
- Using the dictionary
- Using context clues

Secondary emphasis

- The sound for *re*
- Vocabulary review (antonyms)
- Review of consonant blends
- Oral reading

Word Chart and Word Meanings

Use the procedure suggested for Lesson 1.

Story

During the preview, review Part 1 of the story and some of the predictions students made about how it would end. Tell students to be alert to clues that will foreshadow the ending as they read Part 2. During the review, help students to understand the story as a whole by reviewing both parts. Then discuss how close students came to predicting the way the story would end. Did any student predict the actual ending? Were they surprised by the ending?

Exercise 2: About the Story

Question 6 provides a good topic for classroom discussion or a longer composition assignment.

Exercise 3: More Work with Consonant Blends and Digraphs

Students are to complete this exercise in the same manner they completed Exercise 3 in the preceding lesson.

Exercise 4: Antonyms

If necessary, remind the student to use process of elimination to complete this exercise.

Exercise 5: Words Beginning with *re-*

Keep in mind that it is the sound *re* that is being emphasized in this lesson. No mention should be made of *re* as a prefix. This only confuses the student.

During the homework preview, it may be necessary to review some of the definitions for the words in the left column. Unless the student is exceptionally motivated, do not demand that he use the dictionary for the troublesome words. The dictionary practice he gets through completing the first exercise is sufficient. Do, however, encourage the student to write brief notes about the troublesome words in the margin so that he can easily recall the meanings of these words when he completes this exercise for homework.

Lesson 7
Review of Consonant Blends: Part 6

Primary emphasis

- Comprehension (written questions and answers)
- Using the dictionary
- Using context clues

Secondary emphasis

- The sound for *re·*
- Syllabication
- Review of consonants and consonant blends
- Oral reading

Word Chart and Word Meanings

Use the procedure suggested for Lesson 1.

Story

Introduce this story by telling students that Guy de Maupassant (1850-1893) was a well-known French writer. Like O. Henry, de Maupassant was noted for his surprise endings. This story is adapted from one of his most famous stories. Tell students to pay close attention to the two women in this story. They should ask themselves "What kind of people are they?" as they read.

During the review, ask students if they guessed how the story would turn out, and if they did, when they first started to suspect the truth. Other questions to discuss or write about are: Do you think Mrs. Carpenter deserved what happened to her? How could the Carpenters have avoided making this mistake? What other lessons can be learned from this story?

Exercise 2: About the Story

The choices for question 10 provide the basis for a good class discussion or brief composition topic in which the students can elaborate upon one of the maxims.

Exercise 4: Consonants and Consonant Blends

In addition to process of elimination and context clues, the student should be encouraged to use word endings as a guide for putting the words in the right places in the sentences.

Exercise 5: Breaking Words Into Syllables

Because of his previous work with syllabication, the student should have no difficulty completing this exercise with the desired accuracy (80% or better).

If the student wishes to use the dictionary to help him complete this exercise, this is perfectly acceptable. Experience indicates that students use the dictionary only for those words that stump them. Please don't worry about dictionary abuse.

Exercise 6: More Words Beginning with *re-*

Again, it is the sound *re* that is being emphasized in this exercise, and no mention should be made of *re* as a prefix. Students are to be encouraged to use the dictionary for this exercise if necessary.

Lesson 8
Review of Vowel Combinations: Part 1

Primary emphasis

- Comprehension (written questions and answers)
- Using the dictionary
- Using context clues

Secondary emphasis

- *Pre-* and *per-* at the beginning of words
- Vocabulary review
- Review of vowel combinations
- Oral reading

Word Chart and Word Meanings

Use the procedure suggested for Lesson 1.

Story

Introduce this story by explaining that Geoffrey Chaucer (c. 1340-1400) is considered one of the greatest poets in English, and he wrote in the 1300s. This story is from his best-known work, "The Canterbury Tales," a collection of stories purportedly told by a group of pilgrims on their way to a shrine in Canterbury, England. This story was called "The Pardoner's Tale" in the original version.

As a follow-up activity, students might look up and report information on Chaucer. They might also enjoy reading some of the other Canterbury tales. There are many easy-to-read collections available.

Exercise 2: About the Story

Students' interpretation of some of these questions may vary. Accept any answer that the student can justify and discuss differences of opinion. Discuss students' answers to questions 5 and 6 in detail. As a follow-up writing activity, have students write alternative endings beginning with the two murderers drinking the unpoisoned wine.

Exercise 3: Review of Vowel Sounds

Most students have no difficulty putting *poise* in the right place in sentence 6, but they do need additional help in understanding the meaning of this word.

Exercise 4: Where Would You Find This?

Spend a few moments reviewing the meaning of words such as *galley, Huron, southpaw,* and *teller.* These words have appeared in earlier books.

Exercise 5: Words Beginning with *pre-*

It is the sound *pre* that is being emphasized, and no mention of *pre* as a prefix should be made.

Exercise 6: Words Beginning with *per-*

After the student has made any necessary corrections on this exercise, plan a brief spelling quiz on *pre* and *per* words to help the student improve his ability to distinguish between these two sounds.

Review: Lessons 1-8

Use the procedure suggested for the previous review. Please note the following:

1. Exercise 4 needs to be previewed more carefully than the other exercises in this review. Use the following procedure during the preview:

   (a) After the student has silently read the directions and studied the example, ask him to explain why *stove* is the correct answer. Most students respond, "I don't know."

   (b) Have the student read the five words aloud in item 1. Some students now see why *stove* is the answer; others are still confused. For those who are confused, have them read the five words aloud again and encourage them to pay attention to both the underlined letters and the sounds they are producing. At this point, most students understand why *stove* is the correct answer.

   (c) If the student still feels somewhat uncertain, have him complete an item or two during the preview.

   (d) Remind all students to say the words aloud and TAKE THEIR TIME when doing this exercise for homework.

   (e) During the homework review, allow some time to review the definitions of a few of the words. For example, *clove, yeast, chap,* and *artery* often need to be briefly reviewed by students.

2. Exercise 5, item 4: If the student chooses *freeway* rather than *turnpike*, which is the correct answer, spend a few moments discussing how he can use the components of a compound word to discern meaning. In other words, the component *free* implies that no toll would be charged. Thus, even if the student does not know the meaning of *turnpike*, he can easily figure out the answer because it is the only logical choice.

3. The last exercise, If You Had the Money, is just for enjoyment. There is no one correct answer for any of the questions. For some students, this exercise provides the basis for an enjoyable composition topic.

Lesson 9
Review of Vowel Combinations: Part 2

Primary emphasis

- Comprehension (written questions and answers)
- Using the dictionary
- Using context clues

Secondary emphasis

- The ending *-er* meaning *person who*
- Review of common word beginnings
- Spelling/reasoning (Can You Crack the Code?)
- Oral reading

Word Chart and Word Meanings

Use the procedure suggested for Lesson 1.

Story

Introduce this story by drawing students' attention to the title and asking students what they think the story will be about. You might suggest students experiment at home with being "blind" by blindfolding themselves and trying to move around and locate things.

During the review, ask students to find clues in the story that help the reader to figure out that Mr. Parsons was blind. Discuss students' answers to Exercise 3. Have students describe the characters of the two men. Ask "What qualities would lead to their different circumstances, even though they had the same handicap?" Also ask students what they think the title means.

Exercise 4: Who Are These People?

During the homework review, mention that *-er* as an ending often indicates a person.

Exercise 6: Can You Crack the Code?

Although this exercise requires quite a bit of work, students generally enjoy it. Suggest that if the student fills in the letters he knows to be correct from the example (onions) and thinks about the different things that can be put on sandwiches, he should have little difficulty completing this exercise. Students may use the dictionary to help them with spellings if they wish.

Lesson 10
Review of *r*-Controlled Vowels

Primary emphasis

- Comprehension (written questions and answers)
- Using the dictionary
- Using context clues

Secondary emphasis

- Compound words
- Work with word beginnings
- Syllabication (divide compound words)
- Oral reading

Word Chart and Word Meanings

Use the procedure suggested for Lesson 1.

Story

This selection is an adapted biographical piece. During the preview, tell students that this reading is about Louis Braille, a blind Frenchman who lived in the 1800s. Point out that a biography is about someone who really lived, while fiction is not. Ask students if they have heard of the Braille system of writing for the blind. If possible, have a sample or two of Braille writing for students to see and feel.

During the review, discuss with students why being able to read and write was so important for blind people. Remind students that there was no radio nor television in Braille's day.

Exercise 3: More Facts about Louis Braille

During the homework preview, tell students to read each entire sentence before attempting to find the correct answer. Tell them that word endings and context clues can help them to decide which word to place in each blank. Also, they don't have to complete the sentences in the order in which they appear. Remind them that checking off words they have used is helpful.

When students have finished filling in the blanks, have them read the entire passage again for comprehension.

Make sure all students are aware of the fact that the dates in parentheses indicate the birth date and death date of Louis Braille's life.

Exercise 4: Compound Words

All students are quite familiar with this type of exercise by now and should experience little difficulty in completing it.

Exercise 5: More Work with Word Beginnings

Students may use the dictionary to help them complete this exercise if necessary. Answers for 5, 8, and 12 are based solely on the student's judgment.

Exercise 6: Syllables

In addition to checking the syllabication during the homework review, spend a few moments reviewing the definitions of any words that continue to confuse the students.

Lesson 11
The Hard and Soft *c*

Primary emphasis

- Comprehension (written questions and answers)
- Using the dictionary
- Using context clues

Secondary emphasis

- Vocabulary review
- The hard and the soft *c*
- Classifying
- Oral reading

Word Chart and Word Meanings

Use the procedure suggested for Lesson 1.

Story

During the preview, point out that, like the story in Lessons 5 and 6, this story is in two parts. Tell students that it is set in an earlier time and that it probably takes place in Sweden, since the author, Selma Lagerlof (1858-1940) was Swedish. Tell students to think about what kind of person the main character is as they read the story. During the review, ask students if they think the old man was foolish to show the peddler where he kept his money. Have students predict what might happen in Part 2.

Exercise 2: About the Story

Students' answers to these questions may vary. Accept any answer that the student can justify. Students' responses to question 6 can provide the basis for further class discussion or a composition topic.

Exercise 3: What Is a Soul?

Students are to complete this exercise using the same procedure they followed for Exercise 3 of Lesson 10.

Exercise 4: Which Answer Fits Best?

If necessary, remind the student to use process of elimination to complete this exercise. Additionally, students may refer to the dictionary if they wish.

Exercise 5: Sounds for *c*

If necessary, have the student complete one or two items during the homework preview.

Exercise 6: Categories

Students experience little difficulty in completing this exercise accurately. The dictionary may be used if necessary.

Lesson 12
The Hard and Soft *g*

Primary emphasis

- Comprehension (written questions and answers)
- Using the dictionary
- Using context clues

Secondary emphasis

- Classifying
- The hard and soft *g*
- *Dis-* at the beginning of the word
- Oral reading

Word Chart and Word Meanings

Use the procedure suggested for Lesson 1.

Story

During the preview, review Part 1 of the story. Also review any predictions students have made about what will happen next. During the review, help students to understand the story as a whole by reviewing both parts. Discuss cause and effect relationships in the plot. Point out one or two to the students and have them find others. Some examples are: the old man was lonely, so he was glad to see the peddler; the money was easy to take, so the peddler stole it; the peddler was afraid he'd be caught, so he got lost in the woods; the ironmaster thought he recognized the peddler, so he invited him to his home.

After going over students' answers to Exercise 3, discuss the characters of these four people. Ask: Which character changes during the story? In what way? What causes the change?

Exercise 2: About the Story

Discuss students' responses to questions 7, 8, and 9. These questions require students to draw conclusions based on inferences rather than on information directly stated in the story.

Exercise 3: Describing the Characters

Remind students to refer to Lesson 11 if necessary for information about the old man.

Exercise 5: Sounds for *g*

If necessary, have the student complete one or two items during the homework preview.

Exercise 6: Words Beginning with *dis-*

Remind the students to use the word endings to help them place the words properly in the sentences.

Review: Lessons 1-12

1. Use the procedure suggested for the previous reviews.

2. For Exercise 5, use the procedure outlined in the review note for Lessons 1-8. Be sure to remind the student to say the words aloud and to take his time as he completes this exercise for homework.

Lesson 13
The Letter *y*

Primary emphasis

- Comprehension (written questions and answers)
- Using the dictionary
- Using context clues

Secondary emphasis

- Common Sayings
- Adding -*y* to words
- Compound words

Word Chart and Word Meanings

Use the procedure suggested for Lesson 1.

Story

During the preview, tell students that a fable is a short tale that teaches a lesson or moral and that Aesop's fables are very well known. Explain that the characters in fables are often animals and that sometimes an animal is associated with a certain human trait.

During the general review, ask students to name a human trait for each animal in these fables. They might be familiar with the phrase "a sly fox." Then discuss the following sayings in relation to these fables: "Don't kill the goose that lays the golden eggs," "Cover your tracks," and "Pull your chestnuts out of the fire."

Students might enjoy reading more fables. Easy-to-read translations of Aesop's fables should be available in your public library. Many students enjoy writing their own fables after having read these selections from Aesop's fables.

Exercise 3: Write Your Own Moral

The answer given in the Answer Key is a reasonable response. Accept all answers that students can justify.

Exercise 4: Adding -*y* to a Word

Remind the students to refer to the examples when completing this exercise for homework.

Exercise 5: More Common Ways of Speaking

Students tend to have more difficulty with these expressions than they have with those in the preceding review. If process of elimination fails them, encourage them to make an intelligent guess for those which have them completely stumped. A score of 11 or more correct responses should be considered an excellent score.

Exercise 6: Compound Words

This exercise is a bit more difficult than previous exercises pertaining to compound words. Remind students to take their time and use process of elimination.

Lesson 14
Double Consonants in the Middle of Words

Primary emphasis

- Comprehension (written questions and answers)
- Using the dictionary
- Using context clues

Secondary emphasis

- Classifying
- The ending -ment
- Decoding words with double medial consonants
- Oral reading

Word Chart

Students need to draw a line between the double consonant only if this helps them to sound out the words.

Story

During the preview, call students' attention to the title and ask them what they think this story will be about. Ask students to recall times or situations in which they were afraid and what it was that made them afraid. During the review, discuss students' reactions to this story. Explore the fact that people can create their own fear and that fear can spoil one's enjoyment of life. As a follow-up composition topic, have students describe a situation in which they were afraid and tell how they dealt with it.

Exercise 3: What Do You Think?

For question 2, explain that Franklin D. Roosevelt was the American president who made this statement and that he was referring to the Great Depression of the 1930's. Many students are not familiar with this period of American history. Any additional information you can provide about this decade—especially pictures—is helpful.

Exercise 4: The City

Some students will need help understanding the meaning of *sculpture*. This word can be briefly discussed during the homework review. Pictures are helpful.

Exercise 5: The Ending -ment

After the student has made any necessary corrections, a brief discussion of city life vs. country life is usually an enjoyable topic.

Lesson 15
Two Consonants in the Middle of Words

Primary emphasis

- Comprehension (written questions and answers)
- Using the dictionary
- Using context clues

Secondary emphasis

- Vocabulary review (synonyms)
- The ending -ness
- Changing the y to i
- General information (American cities)
- Oral reading

Word Chart

Students need to draw a line between the middle consonants only if this helps them to sound out the words.

Story

During the preview, tell students that "The Streets of Memphis" is part of an autobiography written by Richard Wright, a prominent black American author who wrote most of his major works in the 1940s and 1950s. Discuss the terms *autobiography* and *biography*. Remind students that the selection about Louis Braille in Lesson 10 was an example of biography. Discuss the meaning of the prefix *auto-* and contrast fiction with biography and autobiography.

Tell students that this selection is another story about living in a city and being afraid, but this story really happened. During the follow-up discussion, have students compare "The Streets of Memphis" and "Terror in the Streets" by listing as many similarities and differences between the two stories as they can think of. They should consider differences in plot and setting, but particularly the differences between the two main characters.

Exercise 2: About the Story

During the homework review, have the students speculate on the reasons Richard Wright may have chosen to write an autobiography. Review the terms *autobiography* and *biography* only if necessary.

Exercise 3: More Work with Synonyms

If necessary, review the definition for *synonym*.

Exercise 6: American Cities

Students often need to use the dictionary to complete this exercise. If necessary, remind the student to look under the cities for the correct answer, not the states. Some students also need help in distinguishing between a city and a state.

If you are fortunate enough to have a map or an atlas, have the students locate the cities and states. Be willing to assist them in doing this. This activity helps some students to understand better that a city is in a state.

Lesson 16
More Work with Two Consonants in the Middle of Words

Primary emphasis

- Comprehension (written questions and answers)
- Using the dictionary
- Using context clues

Secondary emphasis

- The endings -*ful* and -*less*
- Homonyms
- Oral reading

Word Chart

Students should draw a line between the two consonants in the middle of the word if this will help them to sound out the words.

Story

During the preview, tell students that this selection, like the one in Lesson 15, is from an autobiography. In "The Thread That Runs So True," poet and writer Jesse Stuart (1907-1984) tells about his years as a teacher. This episode takes place a week after Stuart began his first job teaching in a one-room country schoolhouse. He chose that particular school because one of the students, a large bully named Guy Hawkins, had beaten up Jesse's sister

when she was the teacher there. Ask students if they have ever been in a situation where they felt forced to fight.

During the review, students might be interested to learn that after Jesse Stuart won the fight with Guy Hawkins, he became a local hero since no one else had been able to beat Guy. Stuart left Lonesome Valley at the end of that school year to continue his own education.

Students often enjoy guessing which state Jesse Stuart lived in. The answer is Kentucky.

As a follow-up discussion or composition topic, students might discuss how they feel about the use of violence to settle differences.

Exercise 2: About the Story

Answers to some of these questions may vary from those in the Answer Key. Accept any answer the student can justify.

Exercise 4: Can You Help Guy with His English?

Approach this exercise in the spirit of enjoyment rather than as a usage exercise. Many students are unfamiliar with the usage principles involved in the corrections. Mention these principles in passing during the homework review, but do not belabor the point. Students working in Book 5 improve their usage of standard English more effectively through the composition work rather than through exercises.

Exercise 5: The Endings -*ful* and -*less*

During the homework review, make sure the student understands the meanings of -*ful* and -*less* when used as suffixes. It is not necessary to introduce the term *suffix*.

Exercise 6: Homonyms

After the student has read the directions during the preview, make sure that he can pronounce and define *homonym*. This is also an appropriate time to review the meanings of *synonym* and *antonym*.

Review: Lessons 1-16

Use the same procedure as you have for previous reviews.

Exercise 5: Find the Quote

During the review, students enjoy swapping tricks they have developed to help them solve the puzzle. They also enjoy hearing any tricks you might have developed for problem-solving.

Lesson 17
Common Word Endings

Primary emphasis

- Comprehension (written questions and answers)
- Using the dictionary
- Using context clues

Secondary emphasis

- Compound words
- Review of sounds
- Oral reading

Word Chart and Word Meanings

Use the procedure suggested for Lesson 1.

Story

During the preview, explain that this story is about boxing and that there are some slang expressions in it. Write the following terms and expressions on the board and ask students if they know what they mean. If not, give them the definitions.

middleweights and light-heavies: boxing weight divisions or classes

purse(s): money offered as a prize for a fight

take a dive: throw a fight, lose on purpose

have a set up: have an opponent throw a fight

soft touch: when a boxer is matched with an inferior opponent who is easy to beat

put down for a ten-count: losing a fight by being knocked down for a count of 10 seconds

punchy: groggy or brain damaged from being punched

billing: listing of participants or performers on promotional materials

a C-note: a one-hundred dollar bill

the button: the point of a chin

During the general discussion, ask students what they think might have happened if Rocco had won the fight.

Exercise 2: About the Story

Students may have different answers to these questions than those given in the Answer Key. Use their answers to stimulate discussion. When discussing question 6, ask if students feel the same way about Rocco as the author does. Discuss what kind of person Rocco is. Also, discuss what students think the title of the story means.

Some students enjoy writing about how much honesty they think is generally present in athletic events.

Exercise 3: Compound Words

If the student seems ready for such an exercise based on previous writing, he often enjoys creating his own sentences in which he uses two or more compound words.

Exercise 4: A Review of Word Sounds

By now, most students can complete this type of exercise with an accuracy rate of 70% or better, which is an acceptable score. A few students have developed the habit of groaning in agony upon noticing a word sound review has been included in the lesson. No matter how often they say the words aloud or how patient they are, they find this type of exercise bewildering. For these students, concentrate on reviewing the meanings of some of the words rather than prolonging their agony.

Exercise 5: If Rocco Had . . .

If necessary, remind the student to use the dictionary to complete those items he doesn't know. The questions involving some knowledge of geography often give students difficulty.

Lesson 18
Common Word Endings

Primary emphasis

- Comprehension (written questions and answers)
- Using the dictionary
- Using context clues

Secondary emphasis

- Vocabulary review
- Oral reading

Word Chart and Word Meanings

Use the procedure suggested for Lesson 1.

Words for Study

Even though one of the exercises in this lesson pertains to *banns*, briefly discuss the definition for this word during the preview.

Story

During the preview, explain that the author of this story lived and wrote in Norway in the 1800s. Have students find Norway on the map. Tell students that this story is about a father whose son dies. Ask if they know anyone who has lost a child. During the general discussion, discuss students' reactions to the story.

Exercise 2: About the Story

Adults, in particular, are often moved by this story and enjoy writing compositions about their own children.

Exercise 3: What Are Banns?

Remind the students to take their time with this exercise; it's not as easy as previous exercises of this nature.

Exercise 4: Word Study

If necessary, students are to refer to the dictionary for definitions of forgotten or unknown words.

Exercise 5: Where Would You Find It?

In this section also, students are to refer to the dictionary if necessary.

Lesson 19
The Sound for *ph*

Primary emphasis

- Comprehension (written questions and answers)
- The sound for *ph*
- Using the dictionary
- Using context clues

Secondary emphasis

- Reading a circle graph
- Classifying
- Vocabulary review
- Oral reading

Word Chart

This marks the first lesson in this reading series in which the sound for *ph* is formally studied. Spend some time on the pronunciation of these words with all students.

Story

Introduce this story by pointing out that it is by O. Henry, who also wrote "After Twenty Years" (Lesson 4). Remind students that O. Henry was famous for his suprise endings and that they should watch for clues that might foreshadow the ending. Note that this is the first part of a two-part story. During the general discussion, ask students about Ben Price: who is he? how did he find out where Jimmy is and what his plans are? Discuss students' predictions about what will happen in Part 2 of the story.

Exercise 4: Subjects for Study

During the homework review, review the definitions for *physics, geography,* and *history*. Students who have not worked in Book 4 often need a brief explanation for

Adolf Hitler's role in history. Briefly review with all students the significance of Jamestown in American history.

Exercise 5: Which Answer Fits Best?

Remind the students to take their time with this section and to work by process of elimination.

Exercise 6: A Circle Graph

Because many students are not familiar with either graphs or per cents, thoroughly preview this exercise. If you think it necessary, have the student complete the first two items in class after he has read the directions and studied the graph.

Lesson 20
Four-Letter Words

Primary emphasis

- Comprehension (written questions and answers)
- Using the dictionary
- Using context clues

Secondary emphasis

- Common expressions
- Pronunciation and syllabication (four-letter words)
- Compound words

Word Chart

This is a difficult word chart for many students. Spend some time on the pronunciation of these words and consider using them as the basis for future spelling tests.

Story

During the preview, review Part 1 of this story and students' predictions about what might happen in Part 2. During the review, help students to understand the story as a whole by reviewing both parts. Discuss how close students came to predicting how the story would develop.

During the follow-up discussion, discuss how Jimmy changes in this story and the reasons for those changes. Allow students to share their ideas about how Annabel and her family would have reacted had the story continued.

Exercise 3: "Heartfelt" Expressions

Remind the student to make an intelligent guess for any items that have him completely stumped.

An appropriate discussion topic during the homework review is to speculate why so many expressions in our language include anatomical terms. Adult students particularly enjoy this type of discussion.

Exercise 4: Valentine's Day Customs of Long Ago

This exercise also provides the basis for many discussion topics. Many students enjoy recalling childhood memories of holidays. Additionally, many students are not aware of holidays and other days of the year which are recognized as special. This is an appropriate time to review such days and briefly discuss their backgrounds.

Exercise 5: Syllables

Students are to be discouraged from using the dictionary to compete this exercise in order to reinforce their ability to pronounce these words properly.

Exercise 6: Compound Words

For this exercise, students may refer to the dictionary if their own knowledge and process of elimination fail them.

Review: Lessons 1-20

The purpose of this review is to give the student one more opportunity to work with many of the words and concepts emphasized in Book 5. As was recommended in the notes for previous reviews, this review should not be perceived as a test.

After any necessary corrections have been made by the student during the homework review, spend some time reviewing and evaluating the student's progress. Many students enjoy perusing the word index because it represents a concrete symbol of accomplishment.

Answer Key for Book 5

Lesson 1

1 Word Meanings
1. yoke
2. mutt
3. decoy
4. veterinarian
5. rind
6. gap
7. vast
8. mane
9. Nile
10. ban
11. gape
12. jiggle

2 About the Story
1. the granddaughter
2. food
3. faking injuries
4. happiness
5. there is no other medicine to give him
6. Grandpa isn't where he is supposed to be
7. She puts Grandpa in bed with his clothes on.
8. amused
9. We don't really know why.
10. in a town

3 Which Word Does Not Fit?
1. picnic
2. veteran
3. jewelry
4. drenched
5. groaned
6. bicycle
7. wonderful
8. expenses
9. humor
10. foolish
11. protect
12. gloomy
13. reply
14. rind
15. cautious

4 Grandpa Celebrates His Good Luck
1. lightheaded
2. madhouse
3. mealtime
4. blueberry
5. buttermilk
6. Moneybags
7. coffeepot
8. potpie
9. bathrobe
10. newspaper

Lesson 2

1 Word Meanings
1. marshmallow
2. torch
3. stag
4. host
5. snitch
6. chuckle
7. chapel
8. yeast
9. wishy-washy
10. stench
11. shipshape
12. shabby

2 About the Story
1. wine
2. flocks, fields, and forests
3. delight
4. He discovers he cannot eat or drink because everything he touches turns to gold.
5. a. Because Bacchus grants him his wish,
   b. Because Midas hates gold,
   c. Because Midas is greedy,
   d. Because Bacchus is a god,
   e. Because Bacchus looks so dirty,
6. Answers will vary.

3 Strange Sentences
1. Charles's, choice, chocolate, cheesecake, changed
2. chairman, chess, cheapskate, checkbook
3. shoved, shiny, shotgun, shelf, shed
4. shortstop, shy, show, she, shortchanged
5. student, studying, States, strange, stuff
6. stage fright, step, stairway, staggered, stage, standstill

4 Synonyms
1. top
2. silly
3. greet
4. neat
5. winner
6. shudder
7. stink
8. steal
9. choke
10. worn-out
11. stare
12. confused

Lesson 3

1 Word Meanings
1. Flattery
2. brittle
3. cleat
4. clover
5. frostbite
6. blubber
7. cruel
8. flatter
9. fraction
10. cling
11. blur
12. fro

2 About the Story
1. huge
2. quick
3. tense
4. Eel
5. robbing a house
6. angry
7. because he really believes he is an officer
8. what you wear affects how you feel about yourself
9. France
10. dance

What do you think?
Answers will vary.

3 More Strange Sentences
1. blond, black, blushed, blurted, blind
2. Clark's, clerk, clammy, clip, cloth
3. crouched, crates, crammed, cramps, crawl
4. flickering, flooded, flung, flashlights, floated
5. Fred, frightened, freeway, freaked, Friday
6. bride, broke, brand-new, breadbox, brother's, bribed

4 Synonyms
1. panhandle
2. slash
3. fringe
4. ban
5. salute
6. haste
7. frosting
8. roost
9. snitch
10. power
11. marsh
12. fret

5 Which Word Fits Best?

1. boxing
2. shaker
3. smell
4. certain
5. spicy
6. chicken
7. kindhearted
8. strength
9. shoplifting
10. beef

Lesson 4

1 Word Meanings

Group A

1. Greenland
2. Glen
3. pliers
4. prime
5. plumber
6. princess
7. strangle
8. strive
9. stride
10. slug

Group B

1. prank
2. grubby
3. glum
4. glittery
5. slope
6. slack
7. grateful
8. prowler
9. prowl
10. grope

2 About the Story

1. a. false ~~West~~   East
   b. true
   c. false ~~crowded~~   empty
   d. true
   e. false ~~five~~   twenty
   f. false ~~restaurant~~   hardware store
   g. false ~~hardware store~~   drugstore
   h. false ~~he is so tall~~   his nose is a different shape
   i. false ~~Baltimore,~~   Chicago
   j. true
   k. false ~~only~~   in part
   l. false ~~always~~   never
2. Answers may vary.

3 Antonyms

1. first-rate
2. comply
3. half-wit
4. host
5. follower
6. shortchanged
7. arrest
8. steady
9. enlarge
10. cheapskate
11. antonym
12. strength

4 Strange Verses

1. glasses, clink, think, slurred, blurred, drink
2. princess, distress, shabby, flabby, squeeze, dress
3. prowler, snatching, crippled, dread, frightened, fled

5 Compound Words

1. butterfly
2. powerhouse
3. grandstand
4. headline
5. spendthrift
6. spellbound
7. colorblind
8. whiplash
9. payroll
10. blowtorch
11. panhandle
12. playpen

Review: Lessons 1-4

1 Answer These Questions

1. bathroom
2. prowler
3. plumber
4. library
5. powerhouse
6. avoid
7. able to see clearly
8. oxen
9. veterinarian
10. 1/5
11. Africa
12. Bacchus

2 Synonyms

1. grubby
2. brim
3. pleasure
4. slack
5. slime
6. doubt
7. equal
8. broth
9. slosh
10. avenue
11. earnings
12. madam

3 Antonyms

1. glum
2. hazy
3. safety
4. brighten
5. marshy
6. strive
7. veteran
8. inner
9. whisper
10. fro
11. equal
12. brushoff

4 Common Sayings

1. chip
2. stitch
3. price
4. choosers
5. Blood
6. sleeve
7. shoe
8. flat
9. cherries
10. glass, stones
11. steel
12. charm
13. streak
14. broth
15. grain

5 Compound Words

1. bloodshed
2. crossroad
3. dropout
4. horseshoe
5. nosebleed
6. shoestring
7. slingshot
8. snowflake
9. switchblade
10. wheelchair
1. aircraft
2. birthstone
3. breakdown
4. drawbridge
5. greenhouse
6. gunshot
7. playmate
8. shoelace
9. stoplight
10. storybook

6 Helping People

1. Sunday
2. rooster
3. refrigerator
4. planets
5. hamburgers
6. Michigan
7. castor oil
8. holidays
9. panhandle
10. temper

Quote: Sometimes the best helping hand you can get is a good firm push.

Lesson 5

1 Word Meanings
1. tollbooth
2. trench
3. drifter
4. thriller
5. tweezers
6. treaty
7. thou
8. thorough
9. mothballs
10. trade-in
11. thigh
12. droop
13. trespass
14. twitch
15. throttle

2 About the Story
1. a. false   George had worked in the jewelry business for at least ten years.
   b. false   Mr. Green is pleased enough with George's work to leave him in charge of the store, but in general he treats George as a beginner.
   c. true
   d. true
   e. true
   f. true
   g. false   George goes to the main branch to get expensive rings.
   h. false   George's smile when he calls in sick leads the reader to believe he has other plans for the day.
   i. false   At the end of this part of the story, George seems pleased with himself.
   j. false   This story does not take place in Denver. Mr. Green is going to Denver.
2. Answers will vary.

3 Consonant Blends and Digraphs
1. Fl, sh, dr, st, cr, tr, br, cl, fr
2. Wh, br, gl, cl, th, pl, fr, st, pr
3. tr, dr, dr, st, sh, fr, st, th, dr
4. th, dr, dr, sh, st, ch, th, tr, sh
5. dr, st, pr, gr, gr, tr, br, th, pl

4 Which Word Does Not Fit?
1. silver
2. limp
3. ivy
4. nails
5. stockings
6. dentist
7. spleen
8. Denver
9. tailor
10. receipt

5 Syllables
1. ar • rest
2. brit • tle
3. frost • bite
4. un • lock
5. part • ner
6. with • draw
7. sil • ver
8. shame • ful
9. tres • pass
10. re • ceipt
11. jig • gle
12. pen • cil
13. joy • ful • ly
14. care • ful • ly
15. in • tel • li • gent
16. there • a • bout

6 Where Can You Find It?
1. bloodshed
2. footpath
3. Paris
4. wheelchair
5. busybody
6. sneakers
7. castor oil
8. Egypt
9. princess
10. buttermilk
11. grandstand
12. stoplight
13. Chicago
14. stench
15. tollbooth

Lesson 6

1 Word Meanings
1. Scotland
2. smock
3. skit
4. swank
5. scarcely
6. swimsuit
7. scab
8. skillet
9. screwball
10. skimp
11. smuggle
12. smother
13. snare
14. scrawl (scribble)
15. scribble (scrawl)

2 About the Story
1. a. He shakes George's hand.   He is pleased with the sale George made to Mr. James.
   b. He orders George about.   He is taking over as the boss.
   c. He fires George.   He tries to put the blame for the robbery on George.
2. The thief has his victims gather things in one place so they will be easy to steal.
3. George needed to spend the day buying phony replacements for expensive jewelry.
4. George recognized the oldest trick in the world and stole the jewelry himself.
5. He will go to California, find a job in another jewelry store, and wait for someone else to pull the same trick.
6. Answers may vary.

3 Consonant Blends and Digraphs
1. st, ch, sn, ch, gr, cr, scr, st, pl
2. pr, ch, ch, sh, fr, fr, gr, dr, st
3. St, cr, gl, fl, st, dr, gl, st
4. th, dr, sh, sn, sw, sw, sh, st
5. gr, sh, scr, ch, pl, sw, th, st, cr

4 Antonyms
1. thorough
2. scarce
3. import
4. melted
5. clumsy
6. joyful
7. unnecessary
8. southwestern
9. skinny
10. grouchy
11. restrain
12. plural
13. shabby
14. thrifty
15. strengthen

5 Words That Begin with re-
1. refunded
2. receipt
3. replied
4. repeated
5. replace
6. refused
7. respect
8. recording
9. rejected
10. regarded
11. restrain
12. retreat

Lesson 7

1 Word Meanings
1. speedway
2. spareribs
3. squash
4. shrubbery
5. squid
6. shriek
7. squad
8. splotch
9. whopper
10. spurs
11. spearmint
12. White House
13. squeamish
14. squawk
15. whop
16. splatter

2 About the Story

1. a	3. d	5. c	7. b	9. c
2. c	4. b	6. a	8. a	10. d

3 If You Were the Author

Answers may vary, but considering she is a self-pitying woman, she will probably be very angry and feel life has been unfair to her.

4 Consonants and Consonant Blends

1. tramp, cramp, stamp, ramp
2. flatter, platter, shattered, splattering
3. scared, glare, dare
4. Drenched, clenched, trenches, stench
5. hitch, switch, twitch, witch, snitched
6. shop, flop, crop, stop, plopping
7. smock, clock, shocked, block, flocked
8. shore, chore, swore
9. glum, humming, drummed, scum
10. brushing, slush, blushed, crush

5 Syllables

1. in • vest • ment
2. flat • ly
3. splen • did
4. re • strain
5. ne • ces • sar • y
6. marsh • mal • low
7. care • less • ly
8. turn • pike
9. vel • vet
10. re • place • ment
11. thick • ness
12. draw • string
13. ex • port
14. a • long • side
15. blub • ber
16. op • por • tu • ni • ty

6 Words Beginning with *re-*

1. revolver
2. reborn
3. reward
4. regret
5. review
6. recline
7. reform
8. revolve
9. reveal
10. recite
11. reflect
12. reverse

Lesson 8

1 Word meanings

1. hound
2. barbecue
3. cue
4. fraud
5. traitor
6. creek
7. creed
8. loophole
9. easygoing
10. taut
11. cleanse
12. vain

2 About the Story

1. Death
2. Since the gold does not belong to them, they don't want to take the chance of being questioned. They might meet more people if they tried to move it during the day.
3. He suggests that they stab the third young man and split the gold between them.
4. He plans to poison the other two.
5. Each would have devised a plan to kill the other.
6. Many students may think that each one got his just due, since each planned a murder.

3 Vowel Sounds

1. crook, creek, croak
2. hound, hind, hand
3. boasted, boost, beast
4. heel, hailstorm, heal
5. groaned, groin, grain
6. poise, peas, pose

4 Where Would You Find This?

1. California
2. concert
3. park
4. ocean
5. cocoa
6. Paris
7. chicken
8. fireplace
9. policeman
10. Washington, D.C.

5 Words Beginning with *pre-*

1. precise
2. prepare
3. pretended
4. preview
5. prescribed
6. prevent
7. present
8. predicted

6 Words Beginning with *per-*

1. perfect
2. per cent
3. performers
4. perfume
5. perspired
6. permitted
7. Perhaps
8. perform

Review: Lessons 1-8

1 Word Study

1. c	4. b	7. b	10. c	13. b
2. d	5. b	8. d	11. a	14. c
3. c	6. a	9. b	12. a	15. c

2 Synonyms

1. permit
2. squawk
3. clinging
4. christen
5. applaud
6. easygoing
7. shriek
8. shriveled
9. perspire
10. snare
11. spun
12. value

3 Antonyms

1. youth
2. begin
3. overjoyed
4. glittery
5. cleansed
6. silent
7. complex
8. skimp
9. recline
10. relaxing
11. eager
12. scarce

4 Word Sounds

1. stove
2. yeast
3. host
4. league
5. childish
6. alongside
7. towel
8. bear
9. playground
10. hound

5 Which Word Fits Best?

1. review
2. leaky
3. disease
4. turnpike
5. fry
6. croak
7. outlaw
8. custard
9. veterinarian
10. Washington, D.C.

6 If You Had the Money...

Answers will vary.

Lesson 9

1 Word Meanings

1. soy
2. lease
3. free-for-all
4. Maine
5. unsuited
6. loot
7. Halloween
8. treason
9. ointment
10. annoy
11. wail
12. cease
13. doubtful
14. frail

2 About the Story

1. on a sidewalk
2. spring
3. insurance
4. he thinks Mr. Parsons might give him more money
5. he has ended up blind, but at least Mr. Parsons can see
6. Marks is screaming
7. successful
8. self-pitying
9. a veteran
10. preacher

3 About the Story

1. Parsons is also blind.
2. Mr. Parsons is ambitious, wanting to be successful in life. Marks, on the other hand, uses his blindness as an excuse.

4 Who Are These People?

1. printer
2. porter
3. looter
4. trespasser
5. treasurer
6. trooper
7. producer
8. rancher
9. jeweler
10. sniper
11. wrestler
12. surfer

5 Common Word Beginnings

1. disappoint
2. impressed
3. results
4. unhealthy
5. income
6. inflate
7. infected
8. unlucky
9. import
10. Answers may vary.

6 Can You Crack the Code?

1. onions
2. mustard
3. mayonnaise
4. pickles
5. ketchup
6. cheese
7. peanut butter
8. jelly
9. jam
10. tomatoes

Lesson 10

1 Word Meanings

1. purple
2. mare
3. nightmare
4. jersey
5. sorehead
6. fern
7. market
8. pore
9. New Jersey
10. stern
11. urgent
12. shirk
13. spar
14. sparkle
15. first aid

2 About the Story

1. school
2. spring
3. he fell asleep in class
4. useless
5. unsuccessful
6. dejected
7. none of the sights from his childhood
8. he had to be cut off from the rest of the world because of his blindness
9. relate to others through the written word
10. keep working even when things seem hopeless

3 More Facts about Louis Braille

Frenchman, system

Paris, accident

1824, fifteen, idea, army, messages

1829, praise, machine

4 Compound Words

1. potholder
2. jellybeans
3. woodchuck
4. bloodhound
5. broomsticks
6. forecasts
7. marketplace
8. butterscotch
9. cottonmouth
10. warehouse
11. silverware
12. postcards

5 Word Beginnings

1. retreat
2. unnecessary
3. unemployed
4. disorderly
5. Answers may vary.
6. discounts
7. recall
8. Answers will vary.
9. impact
10. respect
11. comply
12. Answers may vary.

6 Syllables

1. treat • ment
2. sick • ness
3. sore • head
4. room • ful
5. re • birth
6. live • stock
7. com • pact
8. mem • ber
9. pro • ject
10. in • sure
11. head • light
12. les • son
13. keen • ly
14. char • coal
15. an • noy
16. ap • point • ment

Lesson 11

1 Word Meanings

1. incision
2. niece
3. casket
4. cinnamon
5. cucumber
6. carrot
7. mercy
8. calf
9. coop
10. deceased
11. Columbus
12. Cincinnati
13. Cuba
14. catchy
15. cuddle
16. incite

2 About the Story

1. a. selling rat traps
   b. begging
   c. stealing
2. The peddler thinks the world dangles riches in front of a person as a temptation but then retrieves them before the person can grasp them.
3. His beliefs are based on his experience.
4. He was lonely.
5. He is tempted by the old man's money, steals it, and then in trying to avoid being caught, he gets lost in the forest.
6. Answers may vary.

3 What Is a Soul?

body

faiths, cleansed

believed, lifetime, example, return, animal

act, next

4 Which Answer Fits Best?

1. waitress is to waiter
2. mad is to red
3. Denver is to Colorado
4. center is to core
5. Edison is to lightbulb
6. English is to muffin
7. spearmint is to chewing gum
8. New Jersey is to the East
9. floss is to teeth
10. alive is to deceased

5 Sounds for c

1. circus (s,k)
2. company (k)
3. cider (s)
4. cough (k)
5. ceiling (s)
6. dunce (s)
7. decide (s,s)
8. curly (k)
9. curdle (k)
10. cancer (k,s)
11. cue (k)
12. force (s)
13. cobweb (k)
14. Cinderella (s)
15. bacon (k)

6 Categories

Silverware
1. fork
2. knife
3. soupspoon
4. teaspoon

First aid
1. cotton
2. gauze
3. ointment
4. tape

Spices
1. cinnamon
2. clove
3. ginger
4. nutmeg

Animal pens
1. cage
2. coop
3. hutch
4. sty

Disasters
1. blight
2. earthquake
3. flood
4. shipwreck

Paper
1. envelope
2. newsletter
3. postcard
4. ticket

Lesson 12

1 Word Meanings

1. gash
2. gingersnap
3. zigzag
4. gerbil
5. fussbudget
6. budget
7. hag
8. gingerly
9. gallbladder
10. goggles
11. Genesis
12. gabby
13. goad
14. gamble
15. gargle

2 About the Story

1. b
2. a
3. c
4. c
5. a
6. c
7. d
8. a
9. c

3 Categories

The peddler
1. bitter
2. friendless
3. tempted

Elizabeth
1. concerned
2. saintly
3. young

The ironmaster
2. hardworking
3. respected
3. wealthy

The old man
1. lonely
2. retired
3. robbed

4 Which Word Does Not Fit?

1. Texas
2. employee
3. splendid
4. camel
5. roadside
6. bile
7. Asia
8. strikeout
9. smuggler
10. you're welcome
11. cranberry
12. smooth
13. loudmouth
14. insult
15. clause

5 Sounds for g

1. garbage (g)
2. guilty (g)
3. ginger (j,j)
4. Chicago (g)
5. gutter (g)
6. gown (g)
7. gorge (j,j)
8. George (j,j)
9. urgently (j)
10. gap (g)
11. gobble (g)
12. gentle (j)
13. drawbridge (j)
14. gauze (g)
15. barge (j)

6 Words Beginning with *dis-*

1. disclosed, disorderly
2. disabled, disperse
3. disgrace, discovery
4. diseased
5. disgracefully
6. disappointed

Review: Lessons 1-12

1 Word Study

1. draft
2. calf
3. type
4. grate
5. drafted
6. stern
7. grated
8. calf
9. stern
10. type

2 Word Study
1. conducted
2. contest
3. presented
4. content
5. project
6. contents
7. project
8. conduct
9. present
10. contested

3 Synonyms
1. shirk
2. coffin
3. gingerly
4. core
5. deceased
6. apiece
7. thrill
8. employ
9. fraud
10. pastime
11. wail
12. disclose
13. strangle
14. frail
15. twirl

4 Antonyms
1. veteran
2. daylight
3. humid
4. diseased
5. disgrace
6. boost
7. gabby
8. insult
9. damage
10. evil
11. heavyset
12. vast

5 Word Sounds
1. Genesis
2. cinnamon
3. groove
4. both
5. hood
6. sty
7. threat
8. receipt
9. surround
10. shriek

6 Common Ways of Saying Something
1. fuse
2. character
3. gab
4. jackpot
5. backfired
6. bush
7. swear
8. disgrace
9. tone
10. sink
11. fuss
12. Greek
13. cooped
14. catchy
15. bounces

Lesson 13
1 Word Meanings
1. rye
2. valley
3. symptom
4. hymn
5. pulley
6. Pyrex
7. cyclone
8. plywood
9. gyp
10. dye
11. lynch
12. recycle

2 About the Fables
1. Greek
2. B.C.
3. other people telling them
4. a lesson
5. Look before you leap.
6. A bird in the hand is worth two in the bush.
7. a fox
8. intelligence

3 Write Your Own Moral
Do not live just for today; consider what you will need in the future.

4 Adding -y to a Word
1. dressy
2. lumpy
3. fuzzy
4. foamy
5. silvery
1. hazy
2. lacy
3. slimy
4. spiny
5. groovy
1. gabby
2. furry
3. baggy
4. spotty
5. witty

5 Common Ways of Speaking
1. flea
2. lobster
3. goat
4. goose
5. butterflies
6. lion's
7. monkey
8. mouse
9. puppy
10. frog
11. shark
12. shrimp
13. ape
14. horses
15. gnats, camels

6 Compound Words
1. sidestepped, housebroken
2. singsong, watchdog
3. bedroom, pigsty
4. highchair, playpen
5. chatterbox, edgewise
6. nitwit, headphones
7. driveway, applesauce
8. pillowcases, teenage

Lesson 14
1 Word Meanings
A.
1. sissy
2. differ
3. terror
4. slugger
5. dizzy
6. error
7. riddle
8. sorrow
9. wiggle
10. tummy
11. litter
12. petty

B.
1. differ
2. littered
3. puzzling
4. shallow
5. goddess
6. sissy
7. petty
8. correct
9. sorrow
10. terror
11. wiggly
12. mellow

2 About the Story
1. b
2. a
3. d
4. d
5. d
6. c
7. b
8. c
9. a
10. b

3 What Do You Think?
1. She realizes that her fears are out of proportion to the actual danger of living in the city.
2. Fears we have surpass the danger we may find ourselves in; if we can overcome fear, we can deal with the danger.

4 **The City**

Movies	Nightclubs
1. previews	1. bartenders
2. screen	2. cocktails
3. tickets	3. jazz
4. ushers	4. waitresses

Museums	Stadiums
1. drawings	1. bleachers
2. guards	2. goal posts
3. paintings	3. locker rooms
4. sculpture	4. scoreboard

5 **The Ending** *-ment*

1. disappointment   6. payments
2. pavement   7. improvement
3. refreshment   8. argument
4. appointment   9. department
5. installment   10. excitement

Lesson 15

1 **Word Meanings**

A. 1. pester   6. seldom
2. pardon   7. admire
3. target   8. rescue
4. ignite   9. witness
5. advance   10. darling

B. 1. pardon   6. ignite
2. survived   7. admired
3. pester   8. advance
4. ignore   9. tender
5. seldom   10. unseen

2 **About the Story**

1. It is possible that Richard was just glad his father was not home to yell at him, and so he didn't stop to think that his father had actually left.
2. His mother needs help. Also she probably suspects that Richard may run into trouble and feels that it is time for Richard to learn to take care of himself.
3. Answers may vary.
4. Answers may vary.
5. This gang is actually dangerous. In "The Terror in the Streets," the gang was not dangerous; the danger existed only in Margaret's mind.

3 **Synonyms**

1. beam   7. idea
2. top   8. scatter
3. buyer   9. cheat
4. selfish   10. bare
5. vast   11. sign
6. fast   12. lesson

4 **The Ending** *-ness*

1. closeness   6. fitness
2. tenderness   7. thoughtlessness
3. carelessness   8. thoughtfulness
4. illness   9. brightness
5. shyness   10. willingness

5 **Changing** *y* **to** *i*

1. friendliness   9. steadiness
2. sloppiness   10. fuzziness
3. heaviness   11. stickiness
4. emptiness   12. grouchiness
5. fussiness   13. sliminess
6. greediness   14. haziness
7. lumpiness   15. costliness
8. roominess   16. pettiness

6 **American Cities**

1. Georgia   9. Michigan
2. New Jersey   10. Hawaii
3. Maryland   11. California
4. Massachusetts   12. Tennessee
5. Illinois   13. Florida
6. Ohio   14. New York
7. Colorado   15. Washington
8. Texas

Lesson 16

1 **Word Meanings**

1. burden   9. slumber
2. obtain   10. harness
3. absent   11. census
4. vampire   12. London
5. ransom   13. Moscow
6. estate   14. persist
7. cactus   15. boycotting
8. canteen   16. hectic

2 **About the Story**

1. Guy refused to settle the matter any other way.
2. earned Guy's respect.
3. after the fight with Mr. Stuart.
4. it is difficult to reason with a person who has made up his mind to fight you.
5. in a country, one-room school house.

3 **Putting Details in Order**

1, 6, 7, 4, 9, 8, 5, 2, 3, 10

4 **Can You Help Guy with His English?**

1. "No, I've never forgotten anything."
2. "And I'm not going to any other school because of you."
3. "Yes, take off that pretty tie, too."
4. "You won fair too."

5 The Endings -ful and -less

A. 1. mindful   5. graceful
   2. willful   6. sorrowful
   3. sinful   7. distressful
   4. rightful   8. meaningful

B. 1. senseless   5. toothless
   2. errorless   6. motherless
   3. ceaseless   7. fruitless
   4. regardless   8. hatless

6 Homonyms

1. seller, cellar   8. great, grate
2. Where's, wears   9. beech, beach
3. Naw, gnaw   10. real, reel
4. heel, heal   11. sight, cite
5. creek, creak   12. lain, Lane
6. Fore, four   13. alter, altar
7. die, dye

Review: Lessons 1-16

1 Word Study

1. sponsor   6. turnip   11. ambush
2. Aesop   7. slugger   12. curfew
3. vulture   8. fable   13. sissy
4. comma   9. haymaker   14. gossip
5. witness   10. grocery   15. mummy

2 Word Study

1. baggy   6. urgent   11. wiggly
2. gabby   7. rarely   12. persisted
3. dizzy   8. lumpy   13. puppet
4. fussy   9. grisly   14. wisdom
5. grateful   10. recycling   15. Dallas

3 Which Word Does Not Fit?

1. band   6. Sunday   11. buttonhole
2. french fries   7. gnaw   12. drugstore
3. vulture   8. goods   13. darling
4. soapy   9. god   14. ambush
5. bathrobe   10. involved   15. tricycle

4 Syllables

1. month • ly   9. ap • ple • sauce
2. lone • some   10. right • ful
3. wig • gle   11. sing • song
4. edge • wise   12. re • gard • less
5. um • pire   13. im • prove • ment
6. sor • row • ful   14. ten • der
7. high • chair   15. care • less • ness
8. sense • less   16. dis • ap • point • ment

5 Find the Quote

1. found   7. tipping
2. rainbow   8. treason
3. nightmare   9. throttle
4. sunburn   10. breadwinner
5. dippers   11. hay
6. underdog

Quote: Two things that are bad for your heart: running up steps and running down people.

Lesson 17

1 Word Meanings

1. tension   6. flannel   11. private
2. lecture   7. scandal   12. pirate
3. funnel   8. knuckle   13. climate
4. hornet   9. nation   14. punish
5. sandal   10. delicate   15. vanish

2 About the Story

1. Uncle Mike wants to make sure Rocco hasn't forgotten that he agreed to take a dive.
2. a. In the first case, Lily's wearing Rocco's old tennis shoes makes him realize he needs to earn more money.
   b. In the second case, Lily's shoes remind Rocco that he and Lily are a team; they support each other.
3. Lily is very good for Rocco. She apparently doesn't complain about their lack of money. And she clearly is supportive of him as she bets the $100 on him when the odds are 8:1.
4. Although he loses the bout, he loses it honestly rather than taking a dive. So he maintains his self-respect.
5. Rocco did not take a dive, even though he took the money. He remained true to his beliefs and, in his own way, he made good.
6. The author respects Rocco. In the last paragraph, he sums up his feelings: "He always did it the hard way; but he did it."

3 Compound Words

1. somehow, honeymoon
2. handwritten, hopscotch
3. quarterback, teamwork
4. countryside, litterbugs
5. teakettle, stepladder
6. quicksand, rattlesnake

4 Word Sounds

1. remains   6. cough
2. preview   7. nook
3. flow   8. dreadful
4. Butch   9. area
5. grudge   10. league

5 If Rocco Had...

1. guilty
2. scandal
3. footwork
4. too risky
5. lawyer
6. an egghead
7. butterfingers
8. yearbook
9. yogurt
10. yoga
11. gardener
12. Atlantic City
13. Ohio
14. Africa
15. Bethlehem

Lesson 18

1 Word Study

A.
1. crevice
2. British
3. mansion
4. talkative
5. vacation
6. relatives
7. scarlet
8. startle
9. sheepish
10. closet
11. passion
12. fantastic

B.
1. furnished
2. sheepish
3. fantastic
4. encourage
5. informal
6. justice
7. talkative
8. sensitive
9. stylish
10. mansion
11. active
12. wrinkled

2 About the Story

1. a. Thor wanted his son baptized.
   b. Thor wanted his son to stand number one when he was confirmed.
   c. Thor wanted the banns published for his son.
   d. Thor wanted to give half his money to the poor.
2. a. Thor's posture is stooped, and he has white hair.
   b. Money is less important to him.
   c. Answers may vary. He will probably do something more spiritual in nature or something associated with charity.
3. Before his son's death, Thor's happiness seemed to depend on material goods and providing his son with the best of everything. After his son's death, he became less concerned with material wealth and more aware of the importance of spiritual happiness. He shows concern for others by giving money to the poor in his son's name.

3 What are Banns?

public, intend, published, church

begun, prevent, bad, members

opportunity, marriage, reason

1200, banns, holy, practiced

4 Word Study

1. permission
2. magical
3. rockets
4. stylish
5. blushed
6. confirmed
7. stumbled
8. situation
9. sensitive to
10. pirate

5 Where Would You Find It?

1. lion
2. dorm
3. hospital
4. hutch
5. tree
6. station
7. Egypt
8. pocketbook
9. pie
10. desert
11. envelope
12. garden
13. country
14. shoes
15. Asia

Lesson 19

1 Word Meanings

1. graph
2. prophet
3. trophy
4. photo finish
5. gopher
6. physician
7. pharmacy
8. phase
9. phantom
10. photography
11. physique
12. physics
13. geography
14. Philadelphia

2 About the Story

1. a
2. b
3. b
4. d
5. d
6. b
7. d
8. c
9. a

3 What Happens Next?

Answers will vary.

4 Subjects for Study

English	Math	Physics
1. authors	1. fractions	1. energy
2. commas	2. numbers	2. force
3. syllables	3. per cents	3. matter
4. writing	4. sums	4. power

Geography	History
1. deserts	1. battles
2. mountains	2. explorers
3. rivers	3. Adolf Hitler
4. valleys	4. Jamestown

5 Which Answer Fits Best?

1. baked goods
2. damage
3. physique
4. wrench
5. justice
6. grassy plain
7. commission
8. guide is to lead
9. closet is to storing
10. fear is to coward

6 A Circle Graph

1. 5%
2. chicken and liver
3. 2; lamb chops and roast beef
4. Five
5. Twice
6. One half
7. Seafood and steak
8. No
9. No
10. Since this graph depicts the relative popularity of his entrees, the manager could use it to decide which items might be dropped from the menu and which types of items, if any, might be added to the menu.

Lesson 20

1 Word Meanings

1. hula
2. ache
3. chef
4. duet
5. oath
6. debt
7. zero
8. Erie
9. poet
10. amen
11. tidy
12. bawl
13. veto
14. omit

2 About the Story

1. He is going to give them to an old friend.
2. He doesn't want to let on that he knows a great deal about safes.
3. Since Jimmy was putting his skills to good use this time and has been a solid citizen for the past year, Ben sees no good being served by arresting him.
4. April probably would have died. Jimmy's guilt at not trying to rescue her may eventually have caused him to leave town. (Other answers are also possible.)
5. Answers may vary. Probably most students will believe that Jimmy's past will make no difference to Annabel and her family.

3 "Heartfelt" Expressions

1. from the bottom of my heart
2. Have a heart
3. Take heart
4. lost his heart to
5. does my heart good
6. after my own heart
7. break my heart
8. heart's not in it
9. set his heart at rest
10. wear your heart on your sleeve

4 Valentine's Day of Long Ago

regarding, mates

warned, unmarried

customs, choice

husbands, bits, scrap, contain

early, keyholes, objects, peep, married

5 Syllables

1. du • ty
2. ha • lo
3. oath
4. di • et
5. na • vy
6. o • men
7. ho • ly
8. ve • to
9. so • lo
10. chef
11. fu • el
12. ech • o

6 Compound Words

1. shortcoming
2. tenderfoot
3. ringleader
4. taskmaster
5. bloodthirsty
6. wedlock
7. evergreen
8. foxholes
9. windpipe
10. sidetracked

Review: Lessons 1-20

1 Twenty Questions

1. Aesop
2. Bacchus
3. Midas
4. Genesis
5. Bethlehem
6. B.C.
7. A.D.
8. George Washington
9. John Adams
10. veto
11. cabinet
12. New York City
13. Philadelphia
14. Atlantic City
15. Germany
16. Thomas Edison
17. Louis Braille
18. boycott
19. physique
20. Banns

2 Word Review

1. plastic
2. ached
3. keen
4. volleyball
5. mercy
6. geography
7. impact
8. spotty
9. precise
10. investment
11. reverse
12. phase
13. persisted
14. petty
15. poise

3 Synonyms

1. soup
2. coffin
3. alter
4. nation
5. brim
6. hoax
7. worry
8. jewel
9. prod
10. error
11. parcel
12. annoy
13. disperse
14. frail
15. marriage

4 Antonyms

1. uncle
2. doubtful
3. blurred
4. scatter
5. cease
6. roomy
7. faultless
8. host
9. petty
10. wealthy
11. absent
12. distressful
13. holy
14. zigzag
15. mountain

5 Homonyms

1. Bye, by
2. inn, in
3. Fill, Phil
4. him, hymn
5. bawl, ball
6. allowed, aloud
7. main, mane
8. read, reed
9. peeked, peaked
10. pore, pour
11. insight, incite
12. soul, sole

6 Word Sound Review

1. against
2. cleanse
3. woody
4. chow
5. double
6. symptom
7. urgently
8. recipe
9. child
10. citizen

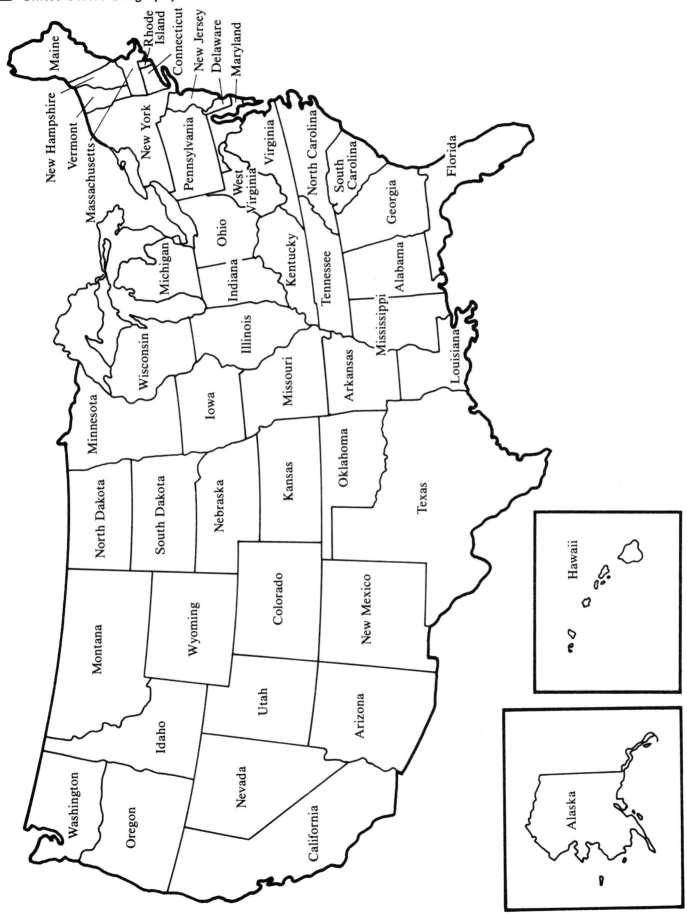

Word Indexes for Book 5

Word Index: Lessons 1–4

A
airtight
antonym
arise
arose
arrest
avenue

B
Bacchus
ban
bathrobe
beech
birthstone
blab
blaze
blessed
blimp
blond(e)
bloodshed
blowtorch
blubber
blueberry
blur
bonnet
bother
boyfriend
brat
breach
breadbox
brighten
brim
brittle
broth
brushoff
buttermilk

C
carefully
castor oil
chairman
champ
chant
chap
chapel
cherry
Chicago

childish
chock
chooser
chuckle
clamp
cleat
clinch
cling
clink
clog
clot
clove
clover
clump
coffeepot
colorblind
contest
cotton
craft
cram
crank
creak
creaky
crest
cripple
crossbar
crossroad
cruel
cuss
custard

D
daze
deathly
decoy
disobey
doubt
drawbridge
dropout

E
earnings
enlarge
equal
equally
eyebrow

F
first-rate
flabby

flatter
flattery
flex
flick
floss
flown
flung
follow
follower
fraction
Fred
fret
fringe
fro
frost
frostbite
frosting
fuzz

G
galoshes
gap
gape
ghost
glassful
glaze
Glen
glider
glittery
glob
glum
granddaughter
grandpa
grandson
grandstand
grasp
grant
grate
grateful
Greenland
grim
grope
grubby
gunshot

H
half-wit
haste

haze
hazy
headline
he's
hitch
horseshoe
host
humid
humor
humorous
hutch

I
inner
insurance
intelligent
interest

J
jig
jiggle
Jimmy
joyfully

K
keen

L
license
lightheaded
lion

M
madam
madhouse
mane
Mars
marsh
marshmallow
marshy
meantime
Midas
mixed
moneybags
mouthpiece
mustard
mutt

N

Nile
nosebleed

O

obey
odds
opening
outburst
outlaw
overpaid

P

palace
Pan
panhandle
panhandler
Paris
partner
payroll
pencil
petal
placement
plainclothes
planter
playmate
playpen
pleasure
pliers
plop
pluck
plumber
potpie
power
powerhouse
prank
pressure
prime
princess
prod
prowl
prowler

Q

quiz

R

ranch
rap
reaction

reorder
rind
roost
rooster
ruby

S

safety
salute
sh!
shabby
shall
shed
shipshape
shiver
shoe
shoelace
shoestring
shoplifting
shortchange
showroom
shudder
slack
slash
slate
slime
slimy
slingshot
slit
slope
slosh
slug
slur
snitch
snowflake
somewhere
solo
spellbound
stab
stack
stag
stagger
steady
steeple
stench
stiff
stole
stoplight
storybook
strangle

strangler
strengthen
strep
stretcher
stride
strive
strut
stub
Susan
switchblade
synonym

T

tango
taxi
they'd
torch
train wreck

U

unequal
uniform
unlighted

V

vast
vent
vet
veteran
veterinarian

W

weakness
welcome
wept
wheelchair
whiplash
whisper
whistle
wick
wishbone
wishy-washy
wit

X

Y

yeast
yoke

Z

zebra

**Word Index:
Lessons 5-8**

A

alongside
applaud
applause
argue
author

B

backward
barbecue
bathmat
boastful
boost
brood

C

carelessly
check-out
Chris
christen
Christ-like
Christopher
chuck
clause
cleanse
cleanser
coldly
company
creed
creek
croak
cue

D

Denver
discussion
draft
drawstring
dredge
drifter
drive-in
droop
druggist
drunken

E
eager
ease
easygoing
envelope
evil
export

F
feedback
flatly
footpath
fountain
fraud
Frenchman

G
gasp
glory
goat
greyhound
groin
groove

H
hailstorm
hardworking
headway
heal
hound

I
impatience
investment
invitation
issue

J
jewel
jeweler

K

L
lain
loafer
loan shark
loin
loop
loophole
Los Angeles

M
master
member
moth
mothball
mount

N
necessary
necklace
northeastern

O
opportunity
outcry
outdoor
overjoyed

P
patience
peak
per cent
perfect
perfume
permit
perspire
pickup
poise
poisoner
pose
post
postman
precise
predict
prepare
prescribe
prevent
preview

Q

R
reborn
receipt
recite
recline
recorder
reed
regret
reload

reminder
replace
replacement
restrain
reverse
review
revolve
revolver
reward
root

S
saint
scab
scalp
scarce
scarcely
schoolhouse
schoolroom
schoolteacher
schooner
Scotland
scramble
scrapbook
scrawl
screwball
scribble
Scripture
scum
self-pity
shriek
shrine
shrivel
shrubbery
shrunken
silver
sketchbook
sketchy
skillet
skim
skimp
skit
smallpox
smelly
smirk
smock
smother
smuggle
snack bar
snare

snazzy
snipe
snowy
snuff
southwestern
spareribs
spearmint
speedway
spike
splashdown
splashy
splatter
spendid
splendidly
splotch
splutter
spotted
sprang
sprig
springtime
sprinkle
spruce
sprung
spun
spur
squad
squash
squawk
squeamish
squid
stock
stringy
suggest
suggestion
swank
sway
sweat shirt
swelling
swimsuit
swollen
swore

T
taut
thank you
thatched
thee
theirs
theme
thereabout

thereafter
they'll
thickness
thigh
thorough
thoroughly
thrash
thresh
thresher
thriller
throttle
throwaway
thruway
tinkle
toad
toilet
toll
tollbooth
totally
tract
trade-in
traitor
treasure
treaty
trench
trespass
troublesome
turnpike
twang
tweed
tweezers
twentieth
twig
twitch

U
unlock
unnecessary
unsteady

V
vain
value
velvet

W
Washington, D.C.
well-to-do
we've

whereabouts
whirlpool
White House
whop
whopper
withdraw
wrestle

X

Y
yours
youth

Z

Word Index: Lessons 9–12

A
ain't
aloud
ankle
annoy
apiece
appoint
appointment
argument

B
battered
beyond
bile
birthplace
blare
blankly
bloodhound
bout
Braille, L.
broomstick
brother-in-law
budge
budget
burnt
butterscotch

C
cabin
cabinet
calf

capital
capitalize
carfare
Carl
carload
carrot
carton
cartoon
cask
casket
catchy
category
cautiously
cease
ceasefire
ceaseless
character
charcoal
cheekbone
Cincinnati
cinnamon
cite
citizen
citizenship
clack
closely
coffin
Colorado
Columbus
compact
coon
coop
core
cottonmouth
Cuba
cucumber
cuddle

D
damage
darkness
day-care
daylight
deceased
decent
decently
decision
deeply

dejected
depression
dirt-cheap
disable
disappoint
disaster
disclose
discomfort
discount
diseased
disgrace
disgraceful
disgracefully
disorderly
disperse
doom
dorm
doubtful

E
earthquake
eastern
effort
eggplant
Elizabeth
employ
employee
engine
engineer
excitement
explosion

F
feature
fellow
fern
first aid
Florida
foam
fore
forecast
forehead
forever
frail
free-for-all
freehand
friendless
frightful

fruitful
fruity
fussbudget

G
gab
gabby
gallbladder
gamble
gambler
gargle
gash
gee-whiz
Genesis
Georgia
gerbil
gifted
gift-wrap
gig
giggle
gingerly
gingersnap
goad
goggles
golf
good-bye
good night
gush

H
hag
Halloween
headlight
head-on
heavyset
highly
hoax
hoot
hotly

I
impact
impossible
incision
incite
indecent
insane
insult
insure

intensely
interesting
ironmaster

J
jag
jagged
jellybean
jersey

K
keenly
kindly

L
lawsuit
lease
livestock
loot
looter
loudmouth
Louis

M
Maine
manage
mare
marker
market
marketplace
mayonnaise
mercy
mill
miscall
mister
moreover

N
Nancy
Neil
New Jersey
niece
nightmare
northern
nutmeg

O
oily
ointment

Olson
orderly

P
package
parson
pastime
peddler
poisonous
pore
porter
possible
postcard
potholder
prison
producer
project
pullover
puppy
purple

Q

R
rancher
ready-made
ready-to-wear
realize
rebirth
recent
repress
roadside
roam
roomful
roomy

S
saintly
shirk
sickness
silverware
sister-in-law
smuggler
sniper
sorehead
soul
southern
soy
spar

sparkle
spy
stern
stolen
straightforward
strikeout
sty
stylus
supper
surfer
surround
system

T
tangle
tempt
thirteenth
thrust
ticket
tobacco
treason
treatment
trespasser
twirl
type

U
unaffected
unemployed
unsuccessful
unsuited
urge
urgent
urgently

V
vat

W
wail
ware
warehouse
wealthy
western
whiner
wildfire
willingness
woodchuck
wooden

workman
wrestler

X

Y

Z
zigzag

Word Index: Lessons 13–16

A
absent
A.D.
address
admire
advance
Aesop
altar
alter
ambush
applesauce
Arizona
arrow
Atlanta

B
banjo
beating
bleacher
blue jay
boldness
boycott
breadwinner
brightness
brisk
briskly
burden
button
buttonhole
buyer
bye
bye-bye
bypass
bystander

C
cactus
canteen

carelessness
census
chatter
chatterbox
clatter
Cleveland
closeness
cocktail
comma
correct
correctly
costliness
coward
crept
curfew
cycle
cyclone

D
Dallas
darling
department
dictionary
differ
difficult
disappointment
distressful
dizzy
dove
dressy
duty
dye

E
edgewise
Edward
elsewhere
emptiness
error
errorless
estate
expression

F
fable
factory
fender
fitness
flatten

foamy
footstep
former
friendliness
fruitless
fumble
furry
fussiness
fuzziness
fuzzy

G
gaily
garlic
gladly
goddess
gossip
greediness
grisly
grocery
groovy
grouchiness
gym
gymnasium
gyp
gypsy

H
handkerchief
harness
hatless
hawk
haymaker
haziness
headphone
heaviness
hectic
highchair
hockey
hollow
homonym
Honolulu
horror
housebroken
hymn
hymnbook

I
ignite
ignore

Illinois
illness
improvement
incorrect
installment
intelligence

J

K
Kenneth
kettle
kidney
kitten

L
ladder
lantern
length
lettuce
litter
London
lonesome
lowland
Lucy
lumber
lumpiness
lumpy
lye
lynch
Lynn(e)

M
mama
Margaret
margin
Maryland
Massachusetts
mattress
meaningful
mellow
Memphis
mental
Miami
mindful
monthly
moral
Moscow

motherless
mummy
mystery

N
napkin
naw
nit
nitwit
nylon

O
oblong
obtain
organ
otherwise
outfielder
overtook

P
parcel
pardon
parent
parrot
pavement
persist
pester
pettiness
petty
pigsty
pillowcase
platform
playroom
ply
plywood
powder
prick
puddle
pulley
puppet
puzzle
Pyrex

Q

R
rabbit
ransom
rattle

recycle
refer
refreshment
regardless
rescue
restore
ribbon
riddle
rightful
roominess
rudely
Russia
rye

S
saleswoman
scatter
scoot
sculpture
Seattle
seldom
seller
senseless
sermon
shallow
shampoo
shyness
sidestep
signal
silvery
singsong
sissy
sliminess
sloppiness
slugger
slumber
snippy
soccer
solve
sorrow
sorrowful
sparrow
spiny
sponsor
spotty
spurt
stark
steadiness
stickiness

stormy
Stuart
style
sunbather
survive
sweetheart
sweetly
symptom

T
tackle
talker
target
teen
teenage
teenager
tender
tenderness
Tennessee
terror
thoughtfulness
thoughtlessness
toothless
treasurer
tricycle
trigger
trumpet
tummy
turnip
typewriter
typewritten
typist

U
umpire
unimportant
unseen
upland
usher

V
valley
vampire
Vermont
volley
volleyball
vulture

W
walnut
walrus

watchdog
wealth
welfare
where's
wiggle
wiggly
willful
wisdom
witness
witty

X

Y
yank
yep

Z

Word Index: Lessons 17-20

A
ache
active
Adams
admission
advantage
ah
aisle
amen
Annabel
anyhow
area
armpit
attend

B
bagpipe
bakery
banns
baptize
barefoot
bawl
beautifully
behalf
Bergman
Bethlehem
billing

bloodshot
bloodstain
bloodthirsty
blowpipe
bobcat
bracket
British
brow
bullet
bumble
burglar
burglary
bury
businessman
buttercup
butterfingers

C
cafe
candle
capture
career
Catholic
checkup
chef
classmate
climate
clinic
closet
combat
combination
commission
commonplace
commotion
compassion
confirm
coolly
countryside
courage
creature
crevice
cricket
Cub Scout
custom

D
damn
data
Dead Sea

deadlock
debt
delicate
detective
diet
direct
discourage
distrustful
downcast
drainpipe
dreamy
dressmaker
duel
duet
dumbbell

E
echo
education
elastic
electric
elephant
emotion
emotional
encourage
enemy
engage
Erie
everglade
evergreen
everlasting
evermore
existence

F
fantastic
faraway
fasten
fifteenth
final
finally
finish
Finn
flannel
flatfoot
flaw
fondly
footwork
formal

fracture
frantic
fuel
funnel
furnish
future

G
garden
gardener
geography
gopher
grandma
graph
gravely
grime

H
halo
handsomely
handwritten
heartfelt
hobo
holy
honest
honeymoon
hopscotch
hornet
hula

I
informal
injustice
inn
invest
Iowa
itchy

J
Jamestown
jungle
justice

K
Karen
kennel
keyhole
knothole
knuckle

L
language
lattice
lecture
lily
litterbug
Little Rock
locket
lotion
lounge

M
magical
mansion
marriage
metal
microphone
middleweight
mission
motion
music
musical

N
nation
navy
needle
needn't
nickel
nightgown

O
oarlock
oath
occasion
omen
omit

P
pal
panel
panic
pantry
passion
permission
personal
phantom
pharmacy
phase
Phil

Philadelphia
Philip
photo
photo finish
photocopy
photograph
photographer
photography
phrase
Phyllis
physic
physical
physician
physique
physics
piecework
pirate
plastic
pocketbook
poem
poet
polite
postmark
postmaster
pothole
powerful
presently
priest
private
promoter
promotion
prophet
public
publish
punchy
punish

Q
quicksand
quietly

R
railing
rainfall
Ralph
rattlesnake
recess
recognize
relationship
relative

relief
relieve
remission
ringleader
ringmaster
ringworm
Rocco
rocket
Rolls Royce
roughly

S
sandal
scandal
scarlet
scoutmaster
section
selection
sensitive
service
setup
sharpen
sheepish
shoehorn
shortcoming
shorthand
shortly
sideline
sideswipe
sidetrack
situation
sixth
skitter
slick
slightly
socket
Solly
somehow
son-in-law
startle
stepladder
storage
strangely
structure
stumble
stylish

T
talkative
taskmaster

tasteful
teakettle
teamwork
tearfully
telephone
tenderfoot
tension
tenth
Thor
thoughtfully
tickle
ticklish
tidy
traffic
trio
trophy
tumble
tunnel

U
unbelievable
uncle
underfoot
unmarried
unpin
Utah

V
vacation
Valentine
vanish
vault
veil
version
veto
vision

W
warden
wedlock
windpipe
wrinkle

X
x-ray

Y
yearbook

Z
zero

Word Index: Lessons 1-20

A
absent
ache
active
A.D.
Adams
address
admire
admission
advance
advantage
Aesop
ah
ain't
airtight
aisle
alongside
aloud
altar
alter
ambush
amen
ankle
Annabel
annoy
antonym
anyhow
apiece
applaud
applause
applesauce
appoint
appointment
area
argue
argument
arise
Arizona
armpit
arose
arrest
arrow
Atlanta
attend
author
avenue

B
Bacchus
backward
bagpipe
bakery
ban
banjo
banns
baptize
barbecue

barefoot
bathmat
bathrobe
battered
bawl
beating
beautifully
beech
behalf
Bergman
Bethlehem
beyond
bile
billing
birthplace
birthstone
blab
blare
blankly
blaze
bleacher
blessed
blimp
bloodhound
blond(e)
bloodshed
bloodshot
bloodstain
bloodthirsty
blowpipe
blowtorch
blubber
blueberry
blue jay
blur
boastful
bobcat
boldness
bonnet
boost
bother
bout
boycott
boyfriend
bracket
Braille, L.
brat
breach
breadbox
breadwinner
brighten
brightness
brim
brisk
briskly
British
brittle

brood
broomstick
broth
brother-in-law
brow
brushoff
budge
budget
bullet
bumble
burden
burglar
burglary
burnt
bury
businessman
buttercup
butterfingers
buttermilk
butterscotch
button
buttonhole
buyer
bye
bye-bye
bypass
bystander

C
cabin
cabinet
cactus
cafe
calf
candle
canteen
capital
capitalize
capture
career
carefully
carelessly
carelessness
carfare
Carl
carload
carrot
carton
cartoon
cask
casket
castor oil
catchy
category
Catholic
cautiously

cease
ceasefire
ceaseless
census
chairman
champ
chant
chap
chapel
character
charcoal
chatter
chatterbox
check-out
checkup
cheekbone
chef
cherry
Chicago
childish
chock
chooser
Chris
christen
Christ-like
Christopher
chuck
chuckle
Cincinnati
cinnamon
cite
citizen
citizenship
clack
clamp
classmate
clatter
clause
cleanse
cleanser
cleat
Cleveland
climate
clinch
cling
clinic
clink
clog
closely
closeness
closet
clot
clove
clover
clump
cocktail
coffeepot

coffin
coldly
Colorado
colorblind
Columbus
combat
combination
comma
commission
commonplace
commotion
compact
company
compassion
confirm
contest
coolly
coon
coop
core
correct
correctly
costliness
cotton
cottonmouth
countryside
courage
coward
craft
cram
crank
creak
creaky
creature
creed
creek
crept
crest
crevice
cricket
cripple
croak
crossbar
crossroad
cruel
Cub Scout
Cuba
cucumber
cuddle
cue
curfew
cuss
custard
custom
cycle
cyclone

D
Dallas
damage
damn
darkness
darling
data
daze
day-care
daylight
Dead Sea
deadlock
deathly
debt
deceased
decent
decently
decision
decoy
deeply
dejected
delicate
Denver
department
depression
detective
dictionary
diet
differ
difficult
direct
dirt-cheap
disable
disappoint
disappointment
disaster
disclose
discomfort
discount
discourage
discussion
diseased
disgrace
disgraceful
disgracefully
disobey
disorderly
disperse
distressful
distrustful
dizzy
doom
dorm
doubt
doubtful
dove

downcast
draft
drainpipe
drawbridge
drawstring
dreamy
dredge
dressmaker
dressy
drifter
drive-in
droop
dropout
druggist
drunken
duel
duet
dumbbell
duty
dye

E

eager
earnings
earthquake
ease
eastern
easygoing
echo
edgewise
education
Edward
effort
eggplant
elastic
electric
elephant
Elizabeth
elsewhere
emotion
emotional
employ
employee
emptiness
encourage
enemy
engage
engine
engineer
enlarge
envelope
equal
equally
Erie
error
errorless

estate
everglade
evergreen
everlasting
evermore
evil
excitement
existence
explosion
export
expression
eyebrow

F

fable
factory
fantastic
faraway
fasten
feature
feedback
fellow
fender
fern
fifteenth
final
finally
finish
Finn
first aid
first-rate
fitness
flabby
flannel
flatfoot
flatly
flatten
flatter
flattery
flaw
flex
flick
Florida
floss
flown
flung
foam
foamy
follow
follower
fondly
footpath
footstep
footwork
fore
forecast
forever

forehead
formal
former
fountain
fraction
fracture
frail
frantic
fraud
Fred
free-for-all
freehand
Frenchman
fret
friendless
friendliness
frightful
fringe
fro
frost
frostbite
frosting
fruitful
fruitless
fruity
fuel
fumble
funnel
furnish
furry
fussbudget
fussiness
future
fuzz
fuzziness
fuzzy

G

gab
gabby
gaily
gallbladder
galoshes
gamble
gambler
gap
gape
garden
gardener
gargle
garlic
gash
gasp
gee-whiz
Genesis
geography

Georgia
gerbil
ghost
gifted
gift-wrap
gig
giggle
gingerly
gingersnap
gladly
glassful
glaze
Glen
glider
glittery
glob
glory
glum
goad
goat
goddess
goggles
golf
good-bye
good night
gopher
gossip
granddaughter
grandma
grandpa
grandson
grandstand
grant
graph
grasp
grate
grateful
gravely
greediness
Greenland
greyhound
grim
grime
grisly
grocery
groin
groove
groovy
grope
grouchiness
grubby
gunshot
gush
gym
gymnasium
gyp
gypsy

H

hag
hailstorm
half-wit
Halloween
halo
handkerchief
handsomely
handwritten
hardworking
harness
haste
hatless
hawk
haymaker
haze
haziness
hazy
headlight
headline
head-on
headphone
headway
heal
heartfelt
heaviness
heavyset
hectic
he's
highchair
highly
hitch
hoax
hobo
hockey
hollow
holy
homonym
honest
honeymoon
Honolulu
hoot
hopscotch
hornet
horror
horseshoe
host
hotly
hound
housebroken
hula
humid
humor
humorous
hutch
hymn
hymnbook

I

ignite
ignore
Illinois
illness
impact
impatience
impossible
improvement
incision
incite
incorrect
indecent
informal
injustice
inn
inner
insane
installment
insult
insurance
insure
intelligence
intelligent
intensely
interest
interesting
invest
investment
invitation
Iowa
ironmaster
issue
itchy

J

jag
jagged
Jamestown
jellybean
jersey
jewel
jeweler
jig
jiggle
Jimmy
joyfully
jungle
justice

K

Karen
keen
keenly
kennel
Kenneth
kettle

keyhole
kidney
kindly
kitten
knothole
knuckle

L

ladder
lain
language
lantern
lattice
lawsuit
lease
lecture
length
lettuce
license
lightheaded
lily
lion
litter
litterbug
Little Rock
livestock
loafer
loan shark
locket
loin
London
lonesome
loop
loophole
loot
looter
Los Angeles
lotion
loudmouth
Louis
lounge
lowland
Lucy
lumber
lumpiness
lumpy
lye
lynch
Lynn(e)

M

madam
madhouse
magical
Maine
mama
manage

mane
mansion
mare
Margaret
margin
marker
market
marketplace
marriage
Mars
marsh
marshmallow
marshy
Maryland
Massachusetts
master
mattress
mayonnaise
meaningful
meantime
mellow
member
Memphis
mental
mercy
metal
Miami
microphone
Midas
middleweight
mill
mindful
miscall
mission
mister
mixed
moneybags
monthly
moral
moreover
Moscow
moth
mothball
motherless
motion
mount
mouthpiece
mummy
music
musical
mustard
mutt
mystery

N

Nancy
napkin

nation
navy
naw
necessary
necklace
needle
needn't
Neil
New Jersey
nickel
niece
nightgown
nightmare
Nile
nit
nitwit
northeastern
northern
nosebleed
nutmeg
nylon

O

oarlock
oath
obey
oblong
obtain
occasion
odds
oily
ointment
Olson
omen
omit
opening
opportunity
orderly
organ
otherwise
outburst
outcry
outdoor
outfielder
outlaw
overjoyed
overpaid
overtook

P

package
pal
palace
Pan
panel
panhandle
panhandler

panic
pantry
parcel
pardon
parent
Paris
parrot
parson
partner
passion
pastime
patience
pavement
payroll
peak
peddler
pencil
per cent
perfect
perfume
permission
permit
persist
personal
perspire
pester
petal
pettiness
petty
phantom
pharmacy
phase
Phil
Philadelphia
Philip
photo
photo finish
photocopy
photograph
photographer
photography
phrase
Phyllis
physic
physical
physician
physique
physics
pickup
piecework
pigsty
pillowcase
pirate
placement
plainclothes
planter

platform
plastic
playmate
playpen
playroom
pleasure
pliers
plop
pluck
plumber
ply
plywood
pocketbook
poem
poet
poise
poisoner
poisonous
polite
pore
porter
pose
possible
post
postcard
postman
postmark
postmaster
potholder
pothole
potpie
powder
power
powerful
powerhouse
prank
precise
predict
prepare
prescribe
presently
pressure
prevent
preview
prick
priest
prime
princess
prison
private
prod
producer
project
promoter
promotion
prophet

prowl
prowler
public
publish
puddle
pulley
pullover
punchy
punish
puppet
puppy
purple
puzzle
Pyrex

Q

quicksand
quietly
quiz

R

rabbit
railing
rainfall
Ralph
ranch
rancher
ransom
rap
rattle
rattlesnake
reaction
ready-made
ready-to-wear
realize
rebirth
reborn
receipt
recent
recess
recite
recline
recognize
recorder
recycle
reed
refer
refreshment
regardless
regret
relationship
relative
relief
relieve
reload
reminder

remission
reorder
replace
replacement
repress
rescue
restore
restrain
reverse
review
revolve
revolver
reward
ribbon
riddle
rightful
rind
ringleader
ringmaster
ringworm
roadside
roam
Rocco
rocket
Rolls Royce
roomful
roominess
roomy
roost
rooster
root
roughly
ruby
rudely
Russia
rye

S
safety
saint
saintly
saleswoman
salute
sandal
scab
scalp
scandal
scarce
scarcely
scarlet
scatter
schoolhouse
schoolroom
schoolteacher
schooner
scoot

Scotland
scoutmaster
scramble
scrapbook
scrawl
screwball
scribble
Scripture
sculpture
scum
Seattle
section
seldom
selection
self-pity
seller
senseless
sensitive
sermon
service
setup
sh!
shabby
shall
shallow
shampoo
sharpen
shed
sheepish
shipshape
shirk
shiver
shoe
shoehorn
shoelace
shoestring
shoplifting
shortchange
shortcoming
shorthand
shortly
showroom
shriek
shrine
shrivel
shrubbery
shrunken
shudder
shyness
sickness
sideline
sidestep
sideswipe
sidetrack
signal
silver

silverware
silvery
singsong
sissy
sister-in-law
situation
sixth
sketchbook
sketchy
skillet
skim
skimp
skit
skitter
slack
slash
slate
slick
slightly
slime
sliminess
slimy
slingshot
slit
slope
sloppiness
slosh
slug
slugger
slumber
slur
smallpox
smelly
smirk
smock
smother
smuggle
smuggler
snack bar
snare
snazzy
snipe
sniper
snippy
snitch
snowflake
snowy
snuff
soccer
socket
Solly
solo
solve
somehow
somewhere
son-in-law

sorehead
sorrow
sorrowful
soul
southern
southwestern
soy
spar
spareribs
sparkle
sparrow
spearmint
speedway
spellbound
spike
spiny
splashdown
splashy
splatter
splendid
splendidly
splotch
splutter
sponsor
spotted
spotty
sprang
sprig
springtime
sprinkle
spruce
sprung
spun
spur
spurt
squad
squash
squawk
squeamish
squid
stab
stack
stag
stagger
stark
startle
steadiness
steady
steeple
stench
stepladder
stern
stickiness
stiff
stock
stole

stolen
stoplight
storage
stormy
storybook
straightforward
strangely
strangle
strangler
strengthen
strep
stretcher
stride
strikeout
stringy
strive
structure
strut
Stuart
stub
stumble
sty
style
stylish
stylus
suggest
suggestion
sunbather
supper
surfer
surround
survive
Susan
swank
sway
sweat shirt
sweetheart
sweetly
swelling
swimsuit
switchblade
swollen
swore
symptom
synonym
system

T
tackle
talkative
talker
tangle
tango
target
taskmaster
tasteful

taut
taxi
teakettle
teamwork
tearfully
teen
teenage
teenager
telephone
tempt
tender
tenderfoot
tenderness
Tennessee
tension
tenth
terror
thank you
thatched
thee
theirs
theme
thereabout
thereafter
they'd
they'll
thickness
thigh
thirteenth
Thor
thorough
thoroughly
thoughtfully
thoughtfulness
thoughtlessness
thrash
thresh
thresher
thriller
throttle
throwaway
thrust
thruway
ticket
tickle
ticklish
tidy
tinkle
toad
tobacco
toilet
toll
tollbooth
toothless
torch
totally

tract
trade-in
traffic
train wreck
traitor
treason
treasure
treasurer
treatment
treaty
trench
trespass
trespasser
tricycle
trigger
trio
trophy
troublesome
trumpet
tumble
tummy
tunnel
turnip
turnpike
twang
tweed
tweezers
twentieth
twig
twirl
twitch
type
typewriter
typewritten
typist

U

umpire
unaffected
unbelievable
uncle
underfoot
unemployed
unequal
uniform
unimportant
unlighted
unlock
unmarried
unnecessary
unpin
unseen
unsteady
unsuccessful
unsuited
upland

urge
urgent
urgently
usher
Utah

V

vacation
vain
Valentine
valley
value
vampire
vanish
vast
vat
vault
veil
velvet
vent
Vermont
version
vet
veteran
veterinarian
veto
vision
volley
volleyball
vulture

W

wail
walnut
walrus
warden
ware
warehouse
Washington, D.C.
watchdog
weakness
wealth
wealthy
wedlock
welcome
welfare
well-to-do
wept
western
we've
wheelchair
whereabouts
where's
whiner
whiplash
whirlpool

whisper
whistle
White House
whoop
whop
whopper
wick
wiggle
wiggly
wildfire
willful
willingness
windpipe
wisdom
wishbone
wishy-washy
wit
withdraw
witness
witty
woodchuck
wooden
workman
wrestle
wrestler
wrinkle

X

x-ray

Y

yank
yearbook
yeast
yep
yoke
yours
youth

Z

zebra
zero
zigzag

NOTES